National Parks in Crisis

Debating the Issues

National Parks in Crisis

Debating the Issues

Wendy Hart Beckman

Enslow Publishers, Inc.

40 Industrial Road	PO Box 38
Box 398	Aldershot
Berkeley Heights, NJ 07922	Hants GU12 6BP
USA	UK

http://www.enslow.com

Library of Congress Cataloging-in-Publication Data

Beckman, Wendy Hart.
   National Parks in crisis : debating the issues / Wendy Hart
Beckman.
      v. cm. — (Issues in focus)
   Includes bibliographical references and index.
   Contents: National parks: yesterday and today— Fire!— Flora and
fauna— Visitors and carrying capacity— Fighting pollution —
Culture clash—Safety and the future.
   ISBN 0-7660-1947-0 (hardcover)
   1. National parks and reserves—United States—Management—
Juvenile literature. 2. United States. National Park Service—Juvenile
literature. 3. Nature conservation—Juvenile literature. [1. National
parks and reserves. 2. United States. National Park Service.
3. Nature conservation.] I. Title. II. Issues in focus (Hillside, N.J.)
SB486.M35B43 2003
333.78'3'0973—dc21

                                              2003006463

Printed in the United States of America

10 9 8 7 6 5 4 3 2 1

To Our Readers: We have done our best to make sure all Internet
Addresses in this book were active and appropriate when we went to
press. However, the author and the publisher have no control over and
assume no liability for the material available on those Internet sites or on
other Web sites they may link to. Any comments or suggestions can be
sent by e-mail to comments@enslow.com or to the address on the back
cover.

Illustration Credits: Ansel Adams/Library of Congress, p. 98;
Ad Council/Forest Service, USDA, p. 34; Wendy Hart Beckman,
pp. 49, 66, 85, 94; © Corel Corporation, pp. 40, 54, 58;
Library of Congress, p. 90; National Park Service, pp. 9, 17, 25,
45, 72, 103. (Note: The name and character of Smokey Bear are
the property of the United States, as provided by 16 U.S.C.
580p-1 and 18 U.S.C. 711, and are used with the permission of
the Forest Service, U.S. Department of Agriculture.)

Cover Illustration: © Corel Corporation.

Contents

Acknowledgments

I would like to thank my family and friends for their support and understanding during the writing of this book, especially my husband, Steve, and my sons, Mark, Christopher, and John. Faculty and participants of the Antioch Writers' Workshop provided motivation and understanding at a crucial time. Of special assistance in the research phase were Bob Miller at Great Smoky Mountains National Park and Lyn Rothgeb at Shenandoah National Park. Superintendents and interpreters at many national parks and other sites were especially encouraging and excited about getting students involved in issues in the national parks. Thanks to Denali National Park and Preserve and Cape Cod National Seashore for providing some of the management documents that govern their activities. Thanks also to Kirk Polking. Finally, I thank my mother and father. Their encouragement started me on my lifelong road to discovery, including a very brief stint with the National Park Service.

1

National Parks: Yesterday and Today

There is a battle ahead on every last frontier. If we lose, America must bid goodbye to what has become a great spiritual and recreational resource. She must give up her living museums of the past, forget the role they play in scientific research. She must abandon forever the part of wilderness in her future economy.

— Sigurd F. Olson, "The Preservation of Wilderness," 1948[1]

On a pristine winter day in Yellowstone National Park, a herd of bison foraged in the snowy landscape as geysers erupted in the background. Just then a whine arose in the distance, growing steadily louder, becoming a deafening screech, accompanied by a cloud of smelly exhaust: snowmobiles!

In February 2003, the administration of President George W. Bush announced that snowmobiles would continue to be allowed on the plowed roads of Yellowstone in the wintertime. This went against a ban on the machines proposed during the Clinton administration. Environmentalists argue that snowmobiles are a source of pollution and danger to animals and people who visit the parks. Park employees have been issued respirators and ear protectors because of the noise and exhaust.

However, snowmobile riders contend that it is the best way to visit Yellowstone in the winter. Cars cannot travel over the snow in the park, and the park is too big for most people to cover on skis or snowshoes. The businesspeople who rent the machines claim that they will go out of business if snowmobiles are banned.

Alternatives to the current situation have been suggested—such as the use of quieter and less polluting snowmobiles or snow coaches, large vans that hold up to ten people. But these solutions do not make everybody happy. Some say the new snowmobiles are not enough of an improvement. Some visitors do not like the snow coaches, finding them slow and boring.[2]

The issue of snowmobiles at Yellowstone illustrates some of the problems facing our national parks today. Many kinds of interests are in conflict: the interests of businesspeople, of animals and plants, of hikers and campers, of those who want to use the

Snowmobilers in Acadia National Park in Maine enjoy the snowy trail. Use of snowmobiles in national parks is a subject of heated debate.

parks today, and of those who want the parks preserved for generations to come.

The national parks of the United States face a number of other issues as well—managing visitors, controlling fires, fighting the effects of pollution, and protecting animals and people from each other. Some of these issues today arose because of decisions made in the past. As people become better educated about cultural and natural resources, it has become clear that some historical actions of the parks' managers were not always in the best interests of the park.

For example, elk were once considered a nuisance in Yellowstone National Park and were routinely removed, hunted, or fenced out. In more recent years, Yellowstone and other parks have even brought elk into the parks in the hopes of returning native species to their original setting. In the twenty-first century, beetles are being introduced in the parks to control the woolly adelgid, an insect pest. Will the beetles become another pest that has to be controlled? Perhaps only time will tell.

But how does one tell what are the best interests of a national park? The mission of the National Park Service (NPS) is to preserve "unimpaired the natural and cultural resources and values of the national park system for the enjoyment, education, and inspiration of this and future generations. The Park Service cooperates with partners to extend the benefits of natural and cultural resource conservation and outdoor recreation throughout this country and the world."[3]

This mission statement means that the Park Service exists to help people enjoy the parks now but also to make sure that the parks are protected so that generations to come can also enjoy the parks. Encouraging people to visit the parks has to be balanced with the possible damage too many visitors might cause, for example.

Not everyone agrees on exactly what is the best way to protect the parks. Not everyone agrees on how the parks should be used. Are burial grounds part of history to be opened and studied? Or are they private and sacred ground to be kept protected and hidden from view? How is a tree better used—by growing tall for people just to look at or by being harvested for lumber to provide homes for families? Should fires from natural sources be allowed to burn, as they would in nature? When do people need to step in to control the burn?

Many of the issues in the national parks today reflect issues in our society in general: pollution, protection of cultural resources, and learning what is of value to us.

What Is a National Park?

There are many types of units in the National Park Service. (For the purposes of this book, the general term "park" will be used to encompass all types.) Many people think of a place of natural beauty when they think of national parks. However, many parks were created because of their cultural or historical significance—for example, Ellis Island and the Statue of Liberty National Monument in New York and George Washington Carver National Monument in Missouri. What sets a national park aside is that it is a place of national significance.

The NPS is an agency under the U.S. Department of Interior. The Park Service, created by act of Congress in 1926, employs more than twenty thousand people with an additional ninety thousand volunteers (people who work without being paid).[4]

National parks protect our natural and cultural resources and processes. Some parks are designated as "wilderness areas." In these areas, the character and resources of wilderness are preserved as if no human had ever touched them. Here, park visitors have to be able to accept the wilderness for what it has to offer without changing it.

Natural resources include physical resources and processes, biological resources and processes, ecosystems, and special natural characteristics that we value (such as scenic views). Physical resources are things you can feel—such as water, air, soil, topographic features (like valleys), geologic features (like rock outcrops), paleontological resources (like fossils); things you can hear—called "soundscapes"; and things you can see—such as clear skies. Physical processes are things that happen, such as the weather, erosion, cave formation, and wildland fires. Biological resources are plants, animals, and their communities. Biological processes are the things that the biological resources do during their lifetimes, such as evolution and photosynthesis. Ecosystems are systems that are formed when organisms interact with their physical environment. Ecosystems contain many species and many processes.

To protect these natural resources, the National Park Service tries to reduce the effects of humans. Any natural processes are left alone, except where they endanger lives or property. Landslides, earthquakes, floods, and fires are examples of some of the natural processes in which the Park Service tries not to interfere.

Areas that have been disturbed or affected by humans are restored to as close to their natural condition as possible. The Park Service uses what is called the "best available technology" to make it look as if technology never had anything to do with it.

The Park Service does many things to erase the evidence of humans. These include:

- Removing exotic (alien) species and restoring native species

- Removing man-made buildings where appropriate

- Restoring areas with abandoned mines or roads to their original condition

- Replanting areas overgrazed by domestic animals such as sheep or cattle

- Restoring areas disturbed by other Park Service activities (such as construction)

- Allowing natural sounds to dominate.[5]

Types of Sites in the National Park Service

The National Park Service oversees national monuments, seashores, recreation areas, historic sites, memorials, battlefields, preserves, waterways, cemeteries, lakeshores, parkways, trails, and affiliated areas. There are also some areas that are one of a kind, such as Wolf Trap Farm Park for the Performing Arts in Virginia.

Altogether, as of January 2003, there were 389 units in the NPS system,[6] covering almost 84 million acres. The largest site is the Wrangell–St. Elias National Park and Preserve near Copper Center,

Alaska. This national park and preserve alone covers more than 13 million acres—an area about the size of Switzerland. All by itself it accounts for over 16 percent of the entire National Park Service system acreage. Thaddeus Kosciuszko National Memorial (honoring a Polish-born Revolutionary War hero) in Philadelphia, Pennsylvania, is the smallest Park Service site—0.02 acres.[7] That is about one tenth the size of a major league baseball diamond.

People sometimes confuse national parks with national forests. The U.S. Forest Service oversees the national forests and is under the Department of Agriculture, a different cabinet office from the Office of the Interior. The rules are different for national parks and national forests. For example, in many national forests, companies are regularly allowed to log trees for timber to make paper and paper products; this is usually not permitted in national parks.

Goals of the National Park Service

Ever since the United States Congress established the first national park—Yellowstone, in 1872—the national parks have confronted challenges. But the challenges of the twenty-first century are different from those faced by the parks in the nineteenth century. And the challenges we deal with today will not be the same as those our grandchildren face.

One of the first goals of park personnel in the 1800s was controlling wildlife and ensuring enjoyable, safe visits for people. However, our definition of "controlling wildlife" has evolved, as in the example of the elk in Yellowstone. The national parks are a kind of mirror for our society. They represent what we consider to be worthy of protection at a given time—and that has changed from age to age.

Who knows what needs to be protected and what is best for the parks? To some extent, people can only guess at what the parks need. We have already affected the parks with our human presence, yet we are trying to maintain the parks in as natural a state as possible while promoting their use and enjoyment by millions of people every year. Sometimes preserving their resources and allowing their use proves to be a difficult balancing act.

Part of the mission of the National Park Service is to work with experts in science and other fields to conduct research in the parks. These partnerships serve several purposes. They help the parks' managers determine what actions to take. They help predict what actions to take at other parks and in other environments. Finally, researchers get information about natural resources and processes in a place where the effects of humans are less than in other areas.

What we do today will one day be history. As the national parks age, future generations of park managers will have to determine whether what was done in the past should be preserved as a part of history. For example, is a building that the NPS put up in the 1920s part of history that should be saved, or is it something that should be torn down when it gets worn out? Park managers—which includes high-ranking officials and technical experts, both in the park itself and in NPS headquarters—must work with the public to make these kinds of decisions.

History of the National Park Service

On March 1, 1872, President Ulysses S. Grant signed the act making Yellowstone National Park. Yellowstone, which covers parts of Montana, Wyoming, and Idaho, was created as a national park long before there was a National Park Service. The park has incredible features, such as waterfalls, geysers, and hot springs. It was clear to most who saw it that Yellowstone's natural resources had to be saved for others to see and enjoy.

The U.S. Congress created the National Park Service in 1916 and placed it under the control of the secretary of the interior. At first, there was no master plan of what national parks would be or how they would be managed. There was no other example to follow, since the concept of national parks was "invented" by the United States. In the more than 130 years since then, many other countries have followed our lead. There are now about twelve hundred national parks and conservation areas in more than one hundred countries around the world.[8]

However, even before the National Park Service was created, Congress and several U.S. presidents thought that it was important to save our natural and cultural resources. On June 8, 1906, President Theodore Roosevelt signed the American Antiquities

Act. The purpose of the Antiquities Act was to protect historical sites, especially Native American structures in the Southwest.[9] This created a special designation of parks called national monuments.

From Yellowstone National Park's beginning in 1872, it fell under the authority of the Secretary of the Interior. However, for thirty-two years, the U.S. Cavalry ran Yellowstone National Park. Because of this, some military influences can still be felt in the

The birthplace of Booker T. Washington, the great African-American leader and educator, is a site of national historical significance, so it is part of the national park system. This is a reconstruction of a cabin on the plantation where Washington was born.

National Park Service of today, such as in the style of the uniforms worn by NPS employees.[10] Having the cavalry run the park was a stroke of genius, since Congress could not decide to what level Yellowstone would be funded. Senator George Graham Vest had inserted a line item in the Sundry Civil Appropriations Bill for 1883 that said the secretary of war could supply men to patrol and guard the park if the secretary of interior felt it necessary. The cavalry also helped cut down on wildlife poaching, which had become a serious problem in Yellowstone. With the U.S. army on the job, visitors to the park finally began to respect the rules protecting the park and its resources.[11]

As of 1915, there were thirteen national parks and eighteen national monuments. Some of the first national parks were Yosemite and Sequoia in California, Mount Rainier in Washington, Crater Lake in Oregon, and Glacier in Montana. The Grand Canyon was made one of the first national monuments by Theodore Roosevelt. It was later made into a national park.[12]

The sites were run inconsistently, and no one seemed to be in charge.[13] On August 25, 1916, President Woodrow Wilson signed into law the National Park Service Organic Act. This act established the National Park Service and stated its mission. The Organic Act said the National Park Service's purpose was to "promote and regulate the use of the . . . national parks . . . which purpose is to conserve scenery and the natural and historic objects and the wild life therein and to provide for the enjoyment of the same in such manner and by such means as will leave them unimpaired for the enjoyment of future generations."[14]

In 1933, during the Great Depression, President Franklin D. Roosevelt created the Civilian Conservation Corps (CCC). The CCC provided jobs for over 2 million men at a time when many families were going hungry because of lack of money and lack of jobs. The CCC built roads and structures, made trails, fought fires, and planted trees. These efforts were considered improvements at the time. In recent years, however, some of their work has been thought of as not as much of an improvement as originally hoped. The important thing at the time was that attention was being paid to the national parks and income was being provided to the workers.

While all this growth was going on in some parks, controversy was stirring in other places. Dinosaur National Monument (in Colorado and Utah) was established in 1915 by President Woodrow Wilson to preserve the beautiful canyons cut out by an ancient stream. However, in the 1930s, the federal Bureau of Reclamation became interested in Echo Canyon in Dinosaur National Monument. They proposed building a dam to provide hydroelectric power.

Many scientists, especially paleontologists, were distressed at the idea of flooding what was the greatest deposit of fossils from the Jurassic period ever discovered up to that time. Many local people saw the canyon as a barren, arid wasteland and were eager to get access to water. Even the Mormons had a stake in the debate, because they felt it was God's will and their mission to create an oasis in the desert. Other great engineering projects were being constructed for the benefit of United States citizens, such as Hoover Dam. These engineering "marvels" were considered a work of beauty in themselves by some. Environmentalists (although the term was not used commonly in that era) felt this was their chance to stop what they could not stop in Yosemite in 1913, when a dam caused the flooding of the beautiful Hetch Hetchy Valley.[15]

Other sites were also acceptable to the Bureau of Reclamation, so the debate seemed to be put to rest until 1950, when newly appointed interior secretary Oscar Chapman raised the idea of a dam again.

Congress held hearings to look at all sides of the case. The Senate passed a bill to authorize construction of the dam. However, people who were opposed to the dam objected strongly. Therefore, the House of Representatives was unable to pass the bill. The battle was resolved for good in 1956 when the members of Congress from Utah and Colorado agreed to delete the dam from the bill. Secretary Chapman agreed.[16]

After World War II, very little money was given to the parks, and they began to fall into disrepair. In 1955, the Park Service started a program referred to as Mission 66 (because it was supposed to be completed by 1966). The goal of Mission 66 was to repair the facilities, fix the roads, and make other needed upgrades.

From the 1970s to the 1990s, the National Park Service began to focus more on the ecological value of the parks rather than just their recreational purpose.[17] National parks had 6 million visitors in 1942, 33 million in 1950, and 72 million in 1960. Then Park Service officials saw the need to limit visitors' access to certain areas so the resources could be protected.

Any attempts to limit use of the parks have been controversial. One example of such a battle was between skiers and the park managers of Mount Rainier National Park in Washington State in the 1940s. Skiers thought money should be spent on additional facilities for winter skiing, while summer visitors did not want the scenery to be marred by lifts that would stand idle in the nonwinter months.

Meanwhile, the concession company that ran the lodges was nearing the end of a long contract. The company's experience had shown them that they would lose money by trying to keep the lodges open in the winter. The park managers did not think they could justify spending money on facilities that would be used only a few months out of the year by just a few people and irritate a lot of people the rest of the year.

The governor of Washington even began to put pressure on the Park Service to improve the skiing facilities. He promised to use state crews to help clear the snow from the roads but withdrew his promise later.

Finally, another ski resort was built just outside the park boundaries. The number of winter visitors to the park fell.[18]

The Park Service has been sued both by groups

who feel they are entitled to use the park their way and by environmental groups who feel the Park Service is not being strict enough. As discussed earlier, the law that governs the National Park Service operations is the Organic Act of 1916. In addition, each park unit has a specific law that established the park and governs its operation. This is called the park's "enabling legislation." When laws are questioned, it is up to the courts to decide what the law intended. This is called interpreting the law. A few key cases have arisen in the last quarter century. Many of them were related to how people want to use the parks and how well the Park Service was protecting the resources. Several cases are especially meaningful.

In the 1980s, a group of commercial fishermen sued the secretary of the interior over Everglades National Park in Florida. The suit challenged the Park Service's practice of closing areas to the public and limiting the harvesting of shellfish. The court ruled that there had, indeed, been evidence of damage to the park's ecosystem. The court also ruled that the Park Service had the right to limit access. The court commended the Park Service's thorough approach to gathering public opinion before taking action.

The National Rifle Association (NRA) also sued the Park Service in the 1980s over limiting hunting and trapping at all national parks. Again, the court ruled that the Park Service was within its rights to limit hunting and trapping (unless a specific park's enabling legislation allowed it). The court, in its ruling, reinforced the preservation intent of the

Organic Act: "The paramount objective of the Park System with respect to indigenous wildlife . . . was, from the beginning, one of protectionism."[19]

Cape Cod National Seashore faced a similar suit from environmental groups over off-road vehicle (ORV) usage. The Park Service felt that ORVs posed a threat to vegetation and took away from the experience of other visitors. Three New England environmental groups felt that the Cape Cod management plan allowed ORVs too much access to the National Seashore.

The court ruled that the plan did protect the National Seashore enough. However, the court declined to rule on whether ORV use could be considered one of the traditional uses referred to in the management plan. The court stated that Cape Cod's enabling legislation, introduced by then-Senator John F. Kennedy, placed the highest priority on "preservation of the Seashore as it existed in 1961."[20] Generally, the court supported the park and its careful decision process behind developing the management plan.

Another challenge in the courts pitted the NPS against the First Amendment to the Constitution of the United States. In 1981, protesters wanted to call attention to the plight of the homeless. The Community for Creative Non-Violence (CCNV) wanted to set up fake homeless tents on the Mall in Washington, D.C. Camping outside designated areas is not allowed by the National Park Service, which is responsible for the Mall, so the request was denied. The CCNV sued, saying the Park Service was violating their right to free speech guaranteed under the First Amendment. The Supreme Court ruled that the Park Service was within its rights to deny the permit.[21] This was an important statement that even when federal statutes seem to clash, the preservation of the national park areas took a high priority.

Rules and Regulations

There are many laws and other regulations guiding management of the national parks. The presidents of the United States have "proclamation authority" under the Antiquities Act of 1906 to establish new national monuments or expand existing ones. Presidents Jimmy Carter and Franklin D. Roosevelt established the most national monuments. President Bill Clinton used his proclamation authority the most to expand existing monuments rather than establish new ones.

Some presidents have used this authority to reduce the size of existing parks, as President Dwight Eisenhower did with Arches National Park in 1960, which had been established as Arches National Monument in 1929 by Herbert Hoover.[22] Before a new park is created, potential sites have to meet very strict criteria, or conditions. Congress has to approve it as well.

Criteria for Creating a National Park

So what does it take for an area to be made into a national park? Usually, the National Park Service first studies proposed additions to the system and then makes recommendations to the secretary of the interior, the president of the United States, and Congress. For the Park Service to make such a recommendation, the prospective site must meet certain conditions.

First, the area must have cultural or natural resources that are of national significance. Second, the site must be a suitable addition to the system. That means that the cultural or natural resources provided by that site are not already in some other existing park. Third, it must be a feasible addition.

Arches National Park in Utah, with its beautiful sandstone formations, was made a national park in 1971; it had been a national monument since 1929.

This means it has to be big enough to be worth protection and to provide enjoyment. It also must be able to be managed by the Park Service at a reasonable cost. Fourth, the proposed park must require management by the National Park Service instead of some other organization. The NPS prefers that sites be governed by local organizations wherever possible. One example of how these conditions work can be seen in what happened with one proposal for a new national park. In 2000, a bill was proposed in the House of Representatives to contribute Park Service funds to establish an interpretive center on the life and contributions of President Abraham Lincoln. The National Park Service opposed the bill, H.R. 3084. In his testimony before the House Subcommittee on National Parks and Public Lands, Associate Director Terrel Emmons noted that the NPS already managed five sites honoring Lincoln: the Abraham Lincoln Birthplace National Historic Site, the Lincoln Boyhood Home National Memorial, the Lincoln Home National Historic Site, Ford's Theatre, and the Lincoln Memorial. In this case, he stated, the proposed center was not a suitable addition because existing parks provided similar cultural resources. Emmons also felt that this site would work better as a site operated by the state, not the federal government.[23]

Once a site has been named a national park, it takes an act of Congress and the president's approval to remove any land from that site. In 1975, Congress removed a large area from Grand Canyon National Park so that it could be added to the Havasupai

Indian Reservation. (Because the Havasupai believe that the Grand Canyon is where the human race began, that land is sacred to them.[24]) A second area of Grand Canyon National Park remained under the Park Service but was made accessible to the tribe for subsistence hunting. ("Subsistence" refers to activities that are necessary for living, rather than just for fun or sport.) Some parks also allow subsistence farming for traditionally associated peoples.[25]

The NPS uses the phrase "traditionally associated peoples" to refer to the first people who either lived in or used an area. They might include

> park neighbors, traditional residents, and former residents who remain attached to a park area despite having relocated. . . . Cultural entities such as tribes, communities, and kinship units are "traditionally associated" with a particular park when (1) the entity regards park resources as essential to its development and continued identity as a culturally distinct people; (2) the association has endured for at least two generations (40 years); and (3) the association began prior to establishment of the park.[26]

Not all "traditionally associated peoples" are of American Indian descent.

The Park Service uses the terms "American Indian" or "Native Americans."[27] Jeanne Marie "Brightfire" Stophlet is the Director of the North American Indian Council. Stophlet advises using the specific tribe or nation, whenever possible, such as "Hopi," "Cherokee," "Inuit," "Seminole," or

"Iroquois." The term "American Indian" will be used in this book to include all such native peoples.

Historical Activities

Activities that took place before a given park was established are often allowed to continue through special arrangement with the government. For example, John D. Rockefeller, Jr., bought a large area of land so that he could donate it to Grand Teton National Park in 1943. President Franklin D. Roosevelt accepted Rockefeller's donation, using it to create Jackson Hole National Monument. This resulted in what has been called "one of the bitterest struggles in the history of the national park and monument system."[28] Cattle owners had used the land for generations for grazing and driving cattle. This activity was not normally allowed in a national park. The cattle ranchers felt that the actions of Roosevelt and Rockefeller had taken away their means of making a living. The Department of Interior "grandfathered" them. (Grandfathering means allowing someone to continue an activity because the activity had been allowed in the past before something changed.) Therefore, the cattlemen were allowed to drive the cattle across national park land for the remainders of the cattlemen's lives.

Besides the cattle ranchers, other people did not like President Roosevelt's action—members of Congress. Congress had already refused to approve Rockefeller's donation and expansion of the monument. Many members of Congress felt that

Roosevelt had misused his power under the Antiquities Act. Congress passed a bill to do away with Jackson Hole National Monument, but Franklin Roosevelt vetoed the bill.[29]

Finally, after fights in Congress and in court, in 1950 parts of Jackson Hole, Wyoming, were added to Grand Teton National Park.[30] However, the president was then forbidden from using the proclamation authority in the state of Wyoming.

Issues Facing the National Parks

On a personal level, our national parks provide excitement and spiritual renewal for many visitors. On a cultural level, they preserve our history and keep safe a physical example of our past. Through the national parks, humans learn that we are merely another type of organism on the planet. But preserving these lands has been, and will continue to be, a challenge.

Even as early as 1925, wilderness advocate Sigurd F. Olson was fighting to keep roads out of the boundary waters area of Minnesota. Olson also successfully led the battle in 1948 against allowing airplanes to fly over the boundary waters area.[31] In 1953, Olson became president of the National Parks Association, a private organization founded in 1919 to protect the interests of the parks. In the 1970s it was renamed the National Parks Conservation Association.[32]

Several national parks have been threatened by the construction of dams. The Glen Canyon National

Recreation Area's Lake Powell was created by damming the Colorado River and flooding the canyon. A Glen Canyon NRA Web page asks two pertinent questions: "What is the price of progress and is it ever too high? What is the legacy we will leave to our children?"[33]

Seven states and Mexico rely on the Colorado River for water. A dam was built in Glen Canyon in Arizona, just upriver from the Grand Canyon, in 1963. As a result, the water's flow was changed. This increased the turbidity, which occurs when sediments get stirred up in the water. The chemistry and temperature of the water also changed drastically. Native fish were almost wiped out. The banks became eroded, and sediments that had been carried down to the beaches were now trapped behind the dam. The Colorado River cannot even make it to the Gulf of California, its original end point, creating ecological problems for that body of water as well. The river now just fades away somewhere in the Mexican desert.

Of other threats to the national parks, some have proceeded but others were fought successfully. Dam construction has been blocked in Dinosaur National Monument (Utah), Kings Canyon National Park (California), Mammoth Cave National Park (Kentucky), Glacier National Park (Montana), and Grand Canyon National Park (Arizona).

The intent of creating parks where natural resources are of national significance is to preserve the site as much as possible. However, because humans are encouraged to recreate in parks, absolute preservation is not possible. "Usufruct" is a strange word that means having the legal right to use and enjoy something that belongs to somebody else, from the Latin words for "use" and "bear fruit." It is a good word to keep in mind while thinking about the national parks. We are all welcome to use the parks, but they do not really belong to us personally. We are stewards of these lands for future generations.

No matter their size and type, many national parks have challenges in common. Visitors and their impacts need to be managed. Native species need to be protected, especially from exotic species (those brought to an area by human activities). Fires must be managed, and the effects of air and water pollution need to be minimized, when possible. The parks must also balance the need for researching and documenting history with the need for respecting the rights of American Indian cultures. As we learn about these issues, we also learn what we can do as individuals to help protect our national parks.

2

Fire!

A radio dispatcher in Shenandoah National Park Headquarters asks a park ranger to give her his location and a report on the fire he is in charge of fighting. Many acres have been burning for days. "I'll have to call you back in a few minutes," the ranger tells the dispatcher, who is passing information between the fire crews and the park superintendent. "I'm hanging on the side of a cliff with one hand and the other hand has the radio. I don't have a hand to look at the map." Drought conditions at the time threatened to turn this major fire

32

into a disaster, but Park Service personnel were able to contain the fire. Soon rain quenched the flames, eased the drought, and lessened the threat of more outbreaks.[1]

A wildfire is burning somewhere in the United States right now. It might have been caused by nature or by carelessness, or it might have been set on purpose. The U.S. Forest Service estimates that there are more than one hundred thousand fires in U.S. forests each year.[2]

Smokey Bear

"Remember—only *you* can prevent forest fires!" This was the motto of Smokey Bear for more than fifty years. (Many people refer to him as "Smokey *the* Bear," but "the" was added for a song; it is not part of Smokey's official name.) Many people still identify this well-loved character with the National Park Service. However, Smokey was really created for the U.S. Forest Service by the War Advertising Council.

During World War II, many people were afraid our enemies would attack our forests to destroy timber needed in the war effort. Smokey Bear was created by the War Advertising Council to raise people's awareness of the need to prevent forest fires. (From 1942 to 1944, the Disney character of Bambi was used.) In 1950, a black bear cub was found badly burned after a fire in the Lincoln National Forest near Capitan, New Mexico. The cub was named Smokey. He became the living animal behind the illustration. Smokey lived at the National

Smokey Bear as been a much-loved symbol for fire safety for over fifty years. Recently, his slogan became "Only you can prevent wildfires!"

Zoo in Washington, D.C., until his death in 1976; he is buried in Smokey Bear Historical State Park near Capitan.[3]

In 2001, the motto was changed to "Only *you* can prevent wildfires!" Wildfires wipe out thousands of acres each year, and the Forest Service felt that individuals needed to be made aware of how often people start these fires. A total area the size of New Hampshire is destroyed each year by wildfires.[4] A wildfire is a forest fire that is burning out of control.

Wildfires can be caused by natural or human forces. Sometimes those human forces are people who start the fires on purpose, with good cause. For example, farmers often use fire to clear their land before planting crops. Fire is gentler on the land than mechanical methods (such as heavy equipment), which compact the soil.

When Is Fire a Good Thing?

Smokey may have done too good a job. There are times where it is not only acceptable to have a fire, but it is also good resource management. In nature, fire occurs frequently through lightning strikes. Fires help clear out and prevent soil-borne diseases and recycle nutrients back into the soil. Despite what some animated movies have shown, most animals escape during a fire. They either outrun it or burrow beneath it.[5]

The Park Service classifies all fires as either wildland fires or prescribed (planned) fires. The term "wildland" fire is often used to distinguish a fire from a structural fire. "Wildland" tends to refer to *what* is burning, and "wildfire" tends to refer to *how* the fire is burning. A wildfire is a fire that is not planned, has escaped control, or is not authorized by state or local regulations.[6] Although different in definition, the two confusingly similar terms— "wildland fire" and "wildfire"—are often used interchangeably.

Wildland fires are fought based on the potential for the fire to damage property or park resources or to harm people. Fighting fires takes a lot of people power and money. The park managers weigh how many natural resources might be consumed by the fire compared to the people and financial resources it would take to fight the fire.

In human attempts to control fire, we mistakenly felt we had to eliminate forest fires completely. Up until the 1940s, fire was seen as a bad thing that had to be avoided and stopped. In the 1950s and 1960s, scientists came to understand that fire plays an important part in the natural cycle of a forest. For example, every one or two hundred years, Yellowstone National Park has a major fire. This is confirmed by studying the growth rings of the trees. In the 1970s, the Park Service adopted a policy of fighting man-made fires, while allowing fires from natural causes to burn unless visitor safety was threatened.

If fires are prevented from happening, a dense amount of forest litter builds up. Then, when a fire erupts—whether natural or through human carelessness—the fire burns hotter and longer and causes more damage. If too many trees are damaged badly, then their roots no longer hold the soil in place. If soil is washed downhill with rains, then the streams receive too much silt. This, in turn, harms the fish and other water organisms.

When small fires occur on a regular basis, the forest litter is cleaned out from under the trees. Some types of lodgepole pine trees have cones that open and deliver their seeds only when heated by fire. This shows us that fire is an important natural process that must be preserved for forest renewal. However, large wildfires might go against park objectives and present a threat to human health and safety. Therefore, fire management policies had to be refined to allow for some types and amounts of fire.

Fire Management Policies

The study of fire and its effects on plant and animal life is called fire ecology. Fires are necessary to the cycle of growth of a forest. Therefore, the Park Service plans "prescribed fires." When the weather conditions are right, a small section of forest is ignited and extinguished after an appropriate amount of time. All prescribed burns have to be planned and approved ahead of time. It confuses some people when forest fires are set on purpose, because it seems to be contrary to what the Park Service stands for. It also upsets people who own property next to a park to see the Park Service setting fires so close to their homes. However, executing a prescribed burn and controlling it can save property owners from losing their houses to a wildfire.

Each park must develop a fire management plan. If those in charge of a park do not have a plan, then they are not permitted to conduct prescribed burns. They must also extinguish all fires, if resources are available.[7]

Famous Fires

The Park Service has dealt with many major fires. From October 25 to 27, 1947, a fire tore through

Acadia National Park near Bar Harbor, Maine. More recently, from April to May 2000, Bandelier National Monument in New Mexico was the site of a major wildfire. This fire had been started by National Park Service personnel to clear out brush. The fire got out of control. Before it could be contained, it destroyed 235 structures and caused the evacuation of twenty thousand people. It also came dangerously close to Los Alamos National Laboratory.[8]

The worst fire in the history of the National Park Service happened in Yellowstone in 1988. A lightning strike in June 1988 caused a fire that soon turned wild. From June to October, about 1.4 million acres burned. It took twenty-five thousand firefighters and $120 million to put out the flames.[9] More than one third of Yellowstone was burned. Not all of the damaged area was forest—meadows and developed areas were damaged as well. Some park roads and facilities were closed during the fire. Of these, sixty-seven buildings were destroyed.[10]

Because lightning caused the Yellowstone fire, the Park Service originally was letting the fire burn itself out. Unfortunately, the fire just spread instead. Finally a drenching rain on September 11, 1988, allowed the firefighters to make a dent in the fire. The snows of November finally extinguished the fires completely.[11]

As is often the case, some good things came from the devastation. The 1989 wildflowers at Yellowstone were said to be the most spectacular in recent memory.

Many environmentalists, visitors, and politicians

have argued about whether the NPS's fire management policy was a good one. An investigation conducted by personnel from the Departments of Interior and Agriculture found the Park Service policies to be sound. However, they recommended that all fire management plans be reviewed and reapproved before any more prescribed burns would be allowed. Finally, the investigation team recommended that fire behavior and effects of the Yellowstone fires should be researched to improve future fire management programs.[12]

Preventing Damage From Wildfires

The best way to fight wildfires is to stop them from happening in the first place. Any ignition source, such as a match, a candle, a cigarette, or a campfire, can start a fire that gets out of control quickly.

All campfires should be extinguished thoroughly. That means water should be poured on the embers of the fire and stirred to make sure the water comes in contact with all the coals. The ashes should be cool to the touch. (It is best to let an adult test this.) To prevent damage to the grass and other plants, fires should be built only in designated fire rings and pits.

All homes should be built a distance away from forests. There should be a "fire break" of at least 30 feet from the home's yard to the stand of trees. (A 100-foot fire break is even better.) When people build their homes near a forest, they should select building materials that are resistant to fire. Existing homes can be treated with fire-retardant chemicals.

Yellowstone National Park was the site of terrible forest fires during the summer of 1988. Over a third of the park land was burned.

("Fire-retardant" means that if the material does catch fire, it burns slowly.) Even the landscaping can be chosen to be resistant to fire. For example, hardwoods are more resistant than the coniferous evergreens—for example, ash is better than pine trees.

Within the 30- to 100-foot safety zone, branches and leaves should be picked up. All trees should be trimmed so that there are no branches below 15 feet. Lawns should be mowed and trees and shrubs pruned regularly. Homeowners should also have a garden hose that can reach every section of the house. Some homeowners whose houses were threatened have kept their houses doused with water.

However, if a wildfire is approaching, everyone needs to listen to the radio and be prepared to leave.

If a wildfire is in the area, the car battery needs to be charged and the car should have a full tank of gas. Cars should be parked facing out of the garage. This is not the time to have a dead battery and be unable to jump it! Another option is to keep the car out in the driveway, pointed in the direction you will drive when you need to evacuate. Pets should be kept in one room, so that they can be located quickly.[13] Finally, a battery-operated radio should be nearby at all times.

From 1991 to 2001, more than 102,000 wildfires were started in the United States through human carelessness. During that same period, only 13,000 were caused by lightning strikes.[14] Our own caution is the best tool we have when it comes to fighting fires: Don't let them start.

3

Flora and Fauna

Animals ("fauna," in Latin) and plants ("flora," in Latin) are a natural part of the experience at the natural resource parks—those parks that are dedicated to preserving areas of natural significance. Interactions between animals and humans can be exciting and fun. However, sometimes these experiences can be unpleasant and even dangerous. People should be careful to plan their visits keeping in mind what plants and animals they might encounter.

For example, bears are common in many of the national parks. Visitors to bear country should be prepared to stow their food when not in use. This means locking it away in a secure place, like the trunk of a car, or suspending it in a special way from a tree.

Loft Mountain campground in Shenandoah National Park used to display a photograph of what a hungry bear can do to a car. Some visitors had ignored the ranger's advice to put their food in the trunk and had kept it inside the vehicle. Unfortunately, the car was a soft-top convertible. The vinyl roof was no match for the black bear's sharp claws.

It is a difficult balancing act, in that the Park Service wants to encourage and enhance sightings of wild animals. However, too-frequent interactions between the same animals and humans can cause an animal to become too dependent or a nuisance.

Even plants can present a challenge. For example, backcountry hikers need to watch for poison ivy and poison oak, of course, but they also need to be on the lookout for woolly adelgid infestations. These white clumps should never be touched because they could be spread to other trees.

Animals and Visitors

If someone brings up the subject of national parks, the first thing you might think of is deer and bears. The next thing you might think of is visitors feeding those deer and bears. According to park rangers, this action is wrong on many levels. First, the wild animals get used to the human food, which is not good for them. Second, they then start hanging around visitor centers and campgrounds hoping for handouts. Unlike Yogi Bear, however, these are not tame cartoon critters looking for "pic-a-nic" baskets. These are wild animals that can kill, which is the third problem with feeding animals. In his book *Guts: The True Stories Behind* Hatchet *and the Brian Books*, writer Gary Paulsen describes seeing a deer maul a child to death right in front of him and the child's mother.[1] Many times parents have foolishly posed their children near these wild animals, forgetting that they are not Bambi or Smokey Bear—rather, they are animals that kill for food or to protect their young.

Rangers at Bryce Canyon National Park (Utah) also tell people not to feed the animals, because feeding can spread disease. Ground squirrels, chipmunks, and prairie dogs can carry hantavirus, a disease currently spreading across the Southwest. Hantavirus, which has killed people in the United States, can be caught by either being bitten by an infected animal or inhaling dust from the animal's fur. Ground squirrels at Bryce have also been known to carry bubonic plague, which is spread by fleas.

Even people who obey the rules can suffer from others' disregard. Visitors to Bryce Canyon have been mobbed by ground squirrels hoping for a handout.[2]

In many human-animal interactions, the person is the one immediately hurt, but the animal almost always loses in the long run. Individual animals that have attacked humans are frequently relocated or euthanized (killed humanely).

This sign in Yosemite National Park has an important reminder for all park visitors.

Interactions with animals can be risky for other reasons. When people stop to feed or photograph the animals, they do not always make sure they are in a safe location. Many car accidents happen because people have stopped their cars on the blind side of a curve or in the middle of the road. Even when people do not stop, the results can be bad. Deer tend to move in groups of two or three, for example. If you see one in the road, there is a good chance that there is another one right behind it. Deer often stand and stare at a moving car and then bolt into the path of the car at the last minute. A deer-car collision can kill a deer and total the car as well. Animal-vehicle interactions have few winners.

Pest Management

Another issue for many national parks is pest management. Pests are defined as living organisms that either interfere with the management objectives of a park or pose a threat to visitor health or safety. The mosquitoes and deer flies sucking your blood might be annoying, but they are not defined as pests. However, if it is determined that those mosquitoes are carrying malaria or West Nile virus, then steps will be taken to control the mosquito population. Exotic pests are controlled through the policies for handling exotic species. Native pests will usually be left alone, unless they threaten any rare or endangered species, cause damage to facilities, or pose a threat to human health and safety.[3] Visitor safety is always a top priority.

Native vs. Exotic Species

A quiet battle rages in almost two hundred of the national parks. Animals and plants that were brought in either on purpose or by accident are displacing the species that belong there. Native species are animals or plants that exist in a location because of natural processes. Exotic species are animals or plants that are in the parks because of human activities. Exotic species are not meant to be there and never were historically. (Exotic species are also called "alien" or "invasive.") These exotic species use resources that the native species needs to survive. This process is called "outcompeting."

In Great Smoky Mountains National Park in Tennessee and North Carolina, streams were stocked with nonnative rainbow trout for better fishing. Unfortunately, the stronger and more aggressive rainbow trout has outcompeted the native brook trout. The rainbows took the food needed by the brook trout and took over their nesting grounds. The brook trout is the only trout species native to the Smokies. Their populations were hurt by logging in the 1930s, pollution, and the competing rainbows. In the 1970s, the Park Service placed a ban on fishing for brook trout in the Smokies. However, through annual fish counts, the Park Service concluded that the fishing ban was not affecting the population of brook trout. In 2002 the ban was lifted for certain streams.[4]

When a native species has been wiped out because of an exotic one, the Park Service considers restoring it to its natural location. The Park Service will try to restore the species if there is enough natural habitat left to support it, if the native species does not pose a threat to human safety, if any other species used to restore the species is genetically similar to the endangered species, and if the original species disappeared because of human effects on its ecosystem.[5]

For example, most stands of American chestnut were wiped out by the chestnut blight, a fungus that attacks the very bottom of the tree trunk. This exotic fungus was accidentally brought in from Asia to the

East Coast of the United States in the early 1900s. When the chestnut trees were killed, the black bears and many other animals lost one of their favorite sources of food. Most of them turned to acorns instead, but researchers believe that the bears thrived better while eating the chestnuts. Most of the chestnuts in the Smokies were wiped out between 1925 and 1940 by the chestnut blight.[6]

For some reason, Chinese chestnut is resistant to the blight. Many researchers are trying to find out what protects the Chinese chestnut so that this same resistance can be genetically "given" to the American chestnut. Any genetic work of this kind uses organisms as closely related to the native organism as possible. This is done for two reasons: so that the research might be more transferable to the species in danger and so that yet another problem will not be introduced by bringing in an exotic species.

Clingman's Dome in Great Smoky Mountains National Park looks as if a horrible fire or ice storm stripped the trees. The culprit is not as large as a fire or a storm, but its effect is far worse. The pest that has caused such serious damage is the woolly adelgid. This tiny insect, native to Asia, is similar to an aphid.[7]

The adelgid burrows into the bark of certain evergreen trees. Adelgid infestation is easily recognizable on trees by the woolly white clump at the base of each needle. The woolly appearance is from a waxy substance the insect coats itself with to keep it from drying out. Starting with the underside of the tree's needles, it sticks its stylet like a wiry probe

Insect pests have taken a toll on this scene at Clingman's Dome, Great Smoky Mountains National Park. The sign shows what the trees used to look like before they were infested with woolly adelgid.

into the bark and sucks sap from the tree. This slows the growth of the tree and causes the needles to fall off. Within two to three years, the tree is dead. Soon the park has a forest of sticks.

The balsam adelgid has destroyed more than 90 percent of the balsam and Fraser firs in the Great Smoky Mountains National Park. The hemlock adelgid has wiped out 80 percent of the hemlocks in Shenandoah National Park. In 2002, the hemlock adelgid was spotted in the Smokies as well.

"Over-visitation or air pollution cannot denude a forest," says Bob Miller of Great Smoky Mountains National Park. "Exotic species can do exactly that."[8]

But the damage is worse than just cosmetic. Hemlocks are important in the natural processes of forests. They provide shade along streams, helping them to keep cool enough to help fish thrive. Freshwater fish are sensitive to changes in temperature. They can even get sunburned without proper shade.

What can be done to save the trees? One small-scale approach is to soak the trees with a soap solution or inject pesticide into the soil. These techniques both have to be applied by hand. A large-scale tactic is the introduction of the Japanese ladybug beetle, which looks like a poppy seed and is a natural enemy of the adelgid. In 2000, five thousand of the beetles, which had been raised in a laboratory, were released in Delaware Water Gap National Recreation Area. They live year-round in the park and have been shown to be the best way to control the hemlock woolly adelgid.[9] In 2002, they were brought into Great Smoky Mountains National Park as well.

On a personal level, as visitors we all need to be careful in handling the trees. If you see a tree that is covered with a white, waxy or woolly-looking substance, do not handle it. If you accidentally touch the infected tree, wash your hands and be careful not to touch any other plants until you do.

One exotic plant that was introduced on purpose is kudzu. Kudzu is a Chinese vine with very broad leaves. It is often planted along roads to stabilize the embankments. Kudzu is used for ground cover—but it works too well. Kudzu is sometimes called "the vine that ate the South," and many southerners joke about kudzu growing over people and pets because they stood still too long. That cannot really happen. But kudzu does, indeed, grow over many things in its path—and that is no joke. Park Service personnel fight the kudzu at their borders to keep it from crossing into park land.

The European wild boar was also brought to the United States on purpose. The hogs were brought into Graham County, North Carolina, to provide stock for hunting in 1912. Unfortunately, the hunters did not get them all. By 1950, the hogs had made it into the Great Smoky Mountains National Park. Now, about five hundred boars still roam the woods of Great Smoky Mountains National Park.[10] They compete with native animals for food. By rooting around in the forests with their noses and tusks, the boars inflict a great deal of damage to the vegetation. Each grown boar eats about fourteen hundred pounds of acorns a year, which are also a food source for many other animals.[11]

The biggest problem with the boars is that they are big and nasty. An adult wild boar can grow as big as four hundred pounds. It has sharp tusks, becomes aggressive when cornered, and frequently kills other animals, including dogs and deer. In fact, the boars present far more of a threat than do the bears that many visitors worry about. However, since the boars are active mostly at night and have a very sharp sense of smell, most visitors never see one.[12] The Park Service is hunting and trapping the boars, but there are more than the Service can keep up with. It is unlikely that the boars will ever be eliminated.

While wild boars were introduced intentionally, one exotic animal whose presence is an accident is the European fire ant, which is causing problems in Acadia National Park. However, like the boar, the ant is unwelcome because of what it does. No one is sure how the ants got in this country. It is a good guess that they were in dirt or plants or boxes that were loaded on European ships and brought to New England. The European fire ants are unwelcome exotics because they are pests, not because they outcompete native ants. The European fire ant bites cause pain and inflammation in a victim. A bite is usually not serious except in babies or the elderly. If many ants were to attack a little child all at once, a serious reaction could occur.[13]

The Park Service has to decide how to manage exotic species. When control of an exotic species is "prudent and feasible," the Park Service will take steps to manage it if it interferes with natural processes, negatively affects the genetic purity of native species, disturbs a cultural landscape or damages cultural resources, or threatens public health and safety.[14]

"Bad" Animals or "Good" Animals?

Public perception has played a large part in protection of animals in national parks. Philetus Norris, the second superintendent of Yellowstone National Park (from 1882 to 1887), had a plan that the park should become an area where animals could be raised for meat. He thought that by making the park's bison a product, the herd could be self-sustaining, paying for their upkeep through the sale of meat and furs.

Other interesting plans were tried at one time or another in the parks, including bringing in animals to create zoos and fencing animals in small pens near the roads so that visitors could see them without getting out of their automobiles.[15]

Who's afraid of the big bad wolf? Today, wolves are seen as beneficial wildlife that must be protected. In fact, the National Park Service is reintroducing wolves to restore parks to a more natural state. But at one time, the managers of many national parks thought the wolves were wiping out other animal populations. They considered any predator animals (those that feed on, hunt, and kill other animals) to be bad. In addition to wolves, that included black bears, grizzly bears, coyotes, mountain lions, and

Wolves were once considered such dangerous predators that people were encouraged to hunt and even poison them. Today they are being reintroduced to some parks.

even pelicans. Superintendent Norris and other park managers encouraged hunters to shoot wolves and to leave poisoned animal carcasses behind for the wolves to eat. By 1880, the wolves were almost completely gone.

In 1883, H. M. Teller, the secretary of the interior, made all sport and subsistence hunting illegal in Yellowstone National Park.[16] However, he did not make fishing illegal.

In 1908, President Theodore Roosevelt sent a letter to Superintendent S.B.M. Young of Yellowstone National Park. "I do not think any more cougars (mountain lions) should be killed in the park," the letter read. Roosevelt noted that naturalists in England had tried to protect the grouse from peregrine falcons. Their attempts had backfired and had proven to be bad for the grouse itself. Nevertheless, between 1900 and 1935, about one hundred wolves, one hundred mountain lions, and four thousand coyotes were killed in Yellowstone National Park by Park Service and army personnel.[17]

Even when humans are not intentionally trying to adjust the numbers of certain species of animals in the park, they have affected the natural organization of animals. One way that this has happened is through the construction of fences, roads, and other barriers that the animals cannot cross during their natural migration patterns. For example, after the 1890s, the elk in Yellowstone park were unable to move from their traditional summer location in the park to their winter locations in the valley outside the park. The valley had become very populated with settlers, and the elk were the victims of fences and hunters. One potential result of their being forced to stay in their summer areas or in close contact with one another is the overgrazing of the land they were confined to.[18]

Big Cypress National Preserve is struggling to protect the Florida panther, one of the most endangered mammals of North America. About eighty to one hundred Florida panthers still exist in the eastern United States. "Big Cypress supports almost half of the population," says Superintendent John J. Donahue. "The major factors in panther population declines are habitat loss, genetic problems due to inbreeding, and traffic fatalities."[19]

When animals or plants are wiped out entirely in a given area, it is called "extirpation." Restoring an extirpated species also restores the niche it occupied in the ecosystem. If the animal or plant population is declining outside the parks also, restoration by the NPS becomes even more crucial.

In 1995, Yellowstone National Park began a program to restore gray wolves to the park. The Yellowstone Gray Wolf Restoration Project moved fourteen wolves into the park from Canada. By December 2002, the Greater Yellowstone Ecosystem (including Yellowstone and Grand Teton National Parks) hosted more than 215 wolves, with about 150 in Yellowstone National Park itself.

An interview with the leader of the project, Mike Phillips, was conducted in January 2003 on National Public Radio. Phillips revealed that the last of the original fourteen wolves had been found dead on

December 31, 2002. "Number 2," as the wolf was
called, had evidently been killed by another pack.
Number 2 and his mate, Number 7, had become the
core of the first naturally formed pack since the start
of the project.[20]

Another example of the Park Service's efforts to
restore native animals is the bighorn sheep. The
bighorn sheep is Colorado's state animal. There are
many types of bighorn sheep, including Rocky
Mountain, Sierra Nevada, Californian, and desert.
(California bighorns are the scarcest of these.) Large
populations of bighorns are shown in the fossil record
of the late Pleistocene Epoch, which began about 1.8
million years ago and ended about eight thousand
years ago. (The epoch that followed the Pleistocene is
the Holocene, or "Recent," which we are still in
today.) Scientists have also found bighorn skeletal
remains and bighorn descriptions in the drawings and
writings of the Pueblo, Anasazi, and Fremont tribes.

Bighorn sheep came close to being wiped out by
competition with domestic sheep and cattle for food
and land and by the diseases carried by domestic
sheep. The places where the bighorns live became
scarcer because of too much grazing and unregulated
hunting, which also affects the vegetation.[21]

In order to restore bighorn sheep to their natural
habitats, bighorns have been taken from some
national parks to others, where the herds are dying
out. One consideration in restoration projects such as
this is the safety of the animals. For example, Sierra
Nevada sheep prefer the east slope of the mountain
ridge of Yosemite National Park (California).

Bighorn sheep, the state animal of Colorado, were nearly wiped out at one point. They are now thriving in several locations in the American Southwest, though they still have a long way to go.

Unfortunately, this slope is outside the boundaries of the park, so the Park Service would not be able to protect the sheep well enough.[22]

Desert bighorns were relocated to Zion National Park in 1973. From 1979 to 1999, desert bighorns were also transplanted to Capitol Reef and Arches National Parks (Utah). An especially good place to see bighorn sheep is the White Rim Trail in Canyonlands National Park in Utah. Canyonlands is an important source of the desert bighorn. For example, forty desert bighorns were taken in 1996 and 1997 to Capitol Reef National Park. Many of the sheep were given radio collars to monitor their health and movements. Much more work remains to be done on this project, but there is not enough money to do so.[23]

The Park Service has partnered with different organizations for other successful restoration projects. Because of these attempts, peregrine falcons have been reestablished in twenty-eight states, including Virginia (Shenandoah National Park), Michigan (Isle Royale National Park), and Colorado (Rocky Mountain National Park). Successful restoration projects include plants, too. The Tennessee purple coneflower has been restored at Stone River National Battlefield in Tennessee.[24]

4

Visitors and Carrying Capacity

*There are many perfectly content with life as
they find it. They will always be the picnickers
and the strollers, and for them are highways,
gravelled trails, and country clubs. For them
scenic vistas of the wild from the shelter of broad
and cool verandas. The others, those who cannot
rest, are of a different breed. For them is sweat
and toil, hunger and thirst, and the fierce
satisfaction that only comes with hardship.*

—Sigurd F. Olson, "Why Wilderness?"
American Forests, September 1938[1]

When the national parks were new at
the end of the nineteenth century, one of
the main goals of the Park Service was to

encourage people to come visit. It worked. The numbers of visitors grew. National parks had 6 million visitors in 1942, 33 million in 1950, and 72 million in 1960; at that point, the NPS began to think seriously about limiting visitors in certain areas. Yellowstone is one area that has experienced very high visitor levels. Yellowstone's 50 millionth visitor entered the park in 1972, exactly one hundred years after the park was established. After only twenty more years, in 1992, Yellowstone's 100 millionth visitor entered the park.[2]

The amount of money that the Park Service receives has not always kept up with increases in visitation levels. Presidents and Congress have supported the parks to different degrees. Congress has not always supplied the funds needed to keep the parks in good shape. As a result, the parks have not always been able to handle the numbers of visitors they receive. This results in a decreased quality of experience for the visitors. It is important, then, to determine a "carrying capacity" for the park based on the ideal of providing visitors with a quality experience while protecting the resources.[3]

Carrying Capacity

Carrying capacity refers to the number of visitors a park is able to handle. It reflects not just the level of visitor use or numbers of visitors, but also the level of activity. Each park superintendent sets the park's carrying capacity, then tries to make sure that the popular areas of the park are not getting more visitors than the limit.[4]

Some parks can easily track the number of visitors. For example, Shenandoah National Park in Virginia has entrance stations at the top and bottom of its 103-mile length. There are two entrance stations in between. Other than these four stations, there is no other paved access by which a visitor can drive into the park. Only backcountry hikers can pass through uncounted and unnoticed, unless they check in with a park ranger, since the Appalachian Trail runs the entire length of Shenandoah, frequently crossing its Skyline Drive.

On the other hand, some parks do not even have entrance stations, or their entrance stations are not open all year round. During the time the stations are closed, no entrance fee is charged and visitors come and go as they please. Shenandoah National Park's Skyline Drive meets with the Blue Ridge Parkway in Waynesboro, Virginia. The Blue Ridge Parkway then continues south until it runs into the Great Smoky Mountains National Park (GSMNP). There is no entrance fee for GSMNP, and there is no fee to drive the Blue Ridge Parkway. It is difficult to count the visitors. However, there are ways. These methods include traffic trip wires, campground and visitor center usage, and surveys. Each park has its own set of counting instructions, developed specifically for that park.

Using these methods, it is estimated that the Great Smoky Mountains National Park is visited more than any other national park in the country.

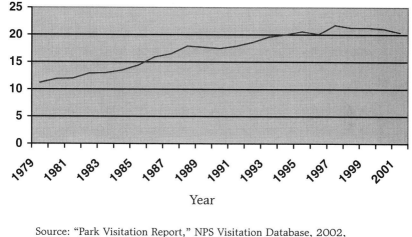

Visitation Report
Great Smoky Mountains National Park

Number of Visits (in millions)

Year

Source: "Park Visitation Report," NPS Visitation Database, 2002,
<http://www2.nature.nps.gov/npstats/parkrpt.cfm> (July 15, 2002).

This park had more than 20 million visitors in 2001 alone. This statistic is not surprising, given that GSMNP is within one day's drive of one third of the population of the United States. With the many state routes crossing the park, many more people pass through the borders than can be counted.

Another park that cannot accurately count its visitors because of the many public roads through the park is Yellowstone National Park. However, it is estimated to have had more than 3.5 million visitors every year since 1994.

More important to the Park Service personnel at

Yellowstone than numbers of visitors is whether or not their budget is enough to cover their expenses. That is, do they receive enough money to keep the facilities of the park in good shape? "We have been known to close an area because of lack of funding," says Marsha L. Karle, Chief of Public Affairs for Yellowstone. "And there was a huge outcry from the public who wished to visit that area."[5]

Lewis and Clark Cavern National Monument was established in 1908 by presidential proclamation. It was transferred to the state of Montana in 1937 by

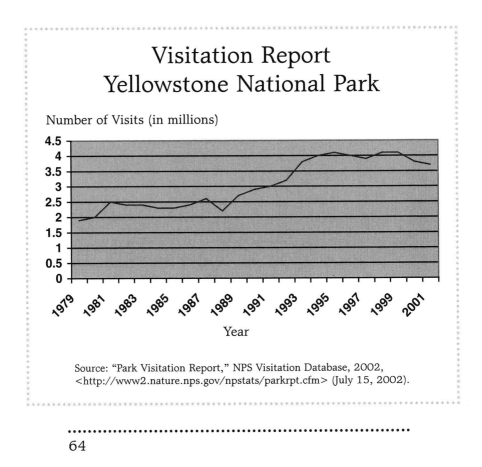

Visitation Report
Yellowstone National Park

Number of Visits (in millions)

Year

Source: "Park Visitation Report," NPS Visitation Database, 2002, <http://www2.nature.nps.gov/npstats/parkrpt.cfm> (July 15, 2002).

an act of Congress. The monument has been closed for years because of lack of funding.

Americans play two roles in this debate: as taxpayers and as potential visitors. People generally do not want tax increases, but they do want the parks to be available to them.

Types of Visitors

What makes a visit to a national park? Does a person have to get out of the car? No, because otherwise many visitors to Pierce Stocking Scenic Drive in Sleeping Bear Dunes National Lakeshore (Michigan), or Skyline Drive in Shenandoah National Park, or the Black Canyon of the Gunnison (Colorado) would not count as visitors. For a long time there has been a tension between those who consider the roads crucial to most visitors' experience of the parks and those who see roads as artificial intrusions upon the land. Sigurd Olson said in a speech to the National Park Service in the mid-1960s that "the automobile is wedded to the American way of life, and Americans are not going to walk, if they can ride."[6]

Visitors to the national parks have different needs and abilities. Elderly visitors might not be able to negotiate trails on foot and might need to rely on access by car. Families with small children might not be able to hike far into the backcountry but might want a campground with bathrooms and tent pads. Some parks have features that allow people of many ages and abilities to enjoy the parks.

What about the people who do get out of their

In Great Smoky Mountains National Park in Tennessee, cars fill the roadside because the parking lots are full. Parking space is often a problem in national parks.

cars? How does their presence affect the park? Acadia National Park in Maine is another park with many public roads running through it. Acadia, like Great Smoky Mountains, does not have entrance stations that are open all year. Charlie Jacobi, a natural resource specialist at Acadia, says that NPS employees at Acadia are concerned about the effects of visitors on plants, animals, soils, and other visitors.[7] One of the ways they manage the visitors' impact is through education. The "Leave No Trace" program educates visitors in how to use a park wisely so that their human impact can be minimized. Unfortunately, visitors to the national parks do not always follow the rules, which can create problems.

Leave No Trace, Inc., is a nonprofit organization whose goal is to help people develop outdoor ethics through education, research, and partnerships. This international program is supported by the U.S. Forest Service, the Bureau of Land Management, the U.S. Fish and Wildlife Service, and the National Park Service.[8] The program lists seven principles for people to follow to make sure they treat nature well. Acadia National Park focuses on two of these principles: (1) travel and camp on durable surfaces and (2) leave what you find. (Acadia has a serious problem with visitors' removing beach cobbles and other rocks and knocking down rock cairns that mark the trails.[9])

The other "Leave No Trace" principles are as follows:

(3) Plan ahead and prepare

(4) Dispose of waste properly

(5) Minimize campfire impacts

(6) Respect wildlife

(7) Be considerate of other visitors

Having too many visitors, especially those who visit from vehicles, causes problems with noise, traffic, and air pollution. In case of too many visitors, the superintendent—the highest ranked official in a park—can choose to close an area, either temporarily or for good; to stop certain activities, such as vehicle traffic; or to control in other ways as he or she deems necessary.

For example, there is a one-way, eleven-mile road in the Great Smoky Mountains National Park. The Cades Cove loop is a very popular drive, with houses and settlements from the early nineteenth century. It is thought to be named after "Kate," the wife of a Cherokee chief. English, Irish, and Scottish settlers came to the area in the 1820s. At its peak in 1850, about 685 people lived in this community. Now over 2 million visitors drive through each year.[10] Cades Cove is one of the most popular sections of the park. During the summer, the road is typically solid with cars and can take up to four hours to travel. One traffic jam caused by deer in the morning can tie up traffic into the afternoon, long after the deer have gone somewhere else.

One solution to the problem is to close the road on certain days or during certain hours, opening up the loop to people who wish to enjoy it on foot or bicycle. GSMNP is conducting a three-year study of vehicle traffic on the Cades Cove Loop. It is not known at this point what the results will be.

In some parks, visitors are encouraged to leave their cars behind to use shuttle buses or other modes of transportation (including their feet). This introduces a secondary problem of where to put the vehicles these visitors leave behind. In some cases, the Park Service creates parking lots and overlooks to accommodate the cars. These paved areas are sited so that they intrude as little as possible upon the natural scenery.

Personal automobiles have been the major form of transportation at most national parks. That will probably not change. However, many parks are looking into alternative transportation systems.[11] For instance, Grand Canyon National Park is considering a light-rail system to be operational in 2004.

Access for Persons with Disabilities

Is it the right of every person to visit a national park? Yes. Is every person able to visit every part of each national park? No. The Park Service tries to make as many areas accessible as possible to a wide variety of people without damaging the resources. Any new developments or facilities are constructed to be fully accessible, as defined by the Americans with Disabilities Act and other regulations.

The Americans with Disabilities Act (ADA) was passed in 1990. One of its goals was to make facilities more accessible to people with disabilities. The National Park Service faces the challenge of balancing the requirements of the ADA with preservation of the characteristic features of its historic properties and its natural parks.[12]

According to NPS policy, in looking at any

changes to a park or site, the Park Service should consider whether the change is

> reasonable, consistent with the preservation of each property's significant historical features. Access modifications for persons with disabilities will be designed and installed to least affect the features of a property that contribute to its significance. . . . However, if it is determined that modification of particular features would impair a property's integrity and character . . . such modifications will not be made.[13]

Many park facilities have been adapted to accommodate people with hearing, sight, and mobility disabilities. In some cases where a site itself cannot be modified enough to accommodate people with disabilities, visitor centers contain mock-ups of the site itself.

Limiting Visitor Services

Early in the development of Yellowstone National Park, it became clear that many visitors wanted places to stay, places to eat, and places to shop. These activities were not part of the mission of the early national park managers. (This was even before the formation of the National Park Service.) Instead, private companies were allowed to come into the park to run these businesses. There have been some problems with the quality and cost of these services, so the government had to take a stronger hand in monitoring how they were run.[14]

One example of these problems concerned E. C. Waters, a concessionaire who ran a steamboat tour business in Yellowstone from 1889 to 1907. He also ran a small zoo on Dot Island, in Yellowstone Lake. One visitor to the zoo reported seeing an elk eating meat, which indicated that it was starving. (Elk are normally herbivores—vegetation eaters.)[15]

The most famous—and perhaps the largest—of the unscrupulous concessionaires of the past was the Yellowstone Park Improvement Company, which turned out to be a front for a group of businessmen out to make a profit from railroads and hotels in the park.[16]

Even more honest concessionaires had some clashes with the Park Service. Wayne Dameron, a concessionaire at North Cascades National Park (Washington), had negotiated a contract in the 1950s and 1960s with the U.S. Forest Service, before the National Park Service took over the park. In 1970, Dameron felt his old contract entitled him to build sixteen floating cabins at May Creek, without having to get permission from the Park Service. His attempt was denied by the superintendent. Dameron was, however, allowed to continue with his existing concession, the Ross Lake Resort.[17]

NPS officials believe that the Park Service juggles the goals of encouraging visitors while protecting the parks from the impacts of those visitors. Some environmental groups would like to see fewer visitors.

Conversely, some visitors would like to see fewer restrictions. Some people would like to be able to have all their needs met within the confines of a national park, including buying gasoline and playing golf. However, the NPS believes that most of these services are better provided outside the park and not inside.[18] In wilderness areas, especially, the NPS thinks that visitors need to enjoy the area on its own terms and not change the wilderness to suit their personal needs—otherwise, it loses its "wild-ness."

In Canyonlands National Park, in Utah, the National Park Service at one time decided that off-road vehicles would be allowed in the streambed of a permanent stream in the park. However, the U.S. District Court in Utah ruled that the Park Service had violated the 1916 National Park Organic Act. The Court said that such use constituted impairment of the park and would have an effect on the resource for

There are many ways to get around in the national parks. These snowshoers are enjoying the winter scenery in Yosemite.

future generations. The Park Service agreed and changed its policy back to forbidding the off-road vehicles in the streambed.[19]

National Park Service Deputy Director Denis P. Galvin testified in July 2000 before the House Subcommittee on National Parks and Public Lands. Galvin's testimony concerned issues involving access to the national parks. Galvin said:

> While providing for visitor use is a fundamental purpose of the Service, units of the National Park System are not simply areas established for recreation. They are places Congress has determined are nationally significant and belong under Federal stewardship. They are areas where we are responsible for protecting wildlife, ecosystems, water quality, and natural quiet; preserving our nation's culture and history; educating visitors; and leaving a legacy of our nation's natural and cultural heritage for future generations. . . . National parks were not intended by Congress to be all things to all people. The growing demand for the more physical forms of outdoor recreational activities on public lands is being met largely by other providers . . . as it should be.[20]

The mood of the Park Service these days is not to encourage high visitation at the most famous parks, such as Yellowstone, Yosemite, and Great Smoky Mountains National Parks, even though fewer visitors would mean less money from visitor fees. However, the NPS is not doing anything to discourage visitation at those parks, either. One of their goals has been to promote the lesser known parks, which would encourage more use by the public and thus decrease overcrowding in the more heavily visited parks.[21] Resources at the heavily visited parks must be protected from current visitors so that future generations will still have parks to visit.

Dave Dahlen, Chief of Interpretation at Glacier National Park, says that parks will always struggle with how much use is too much. He states:

> Too many visitors? Well, uninformed, unaccountable, and uncaring visitors can become a problem. When the opposite happens, we not only create gentler users of the park, but send away people that will better understand their personal relationship to this and other sites. It can be a win-win.[22]

5

Fighting Pollution

Pollution comes in many forms. Air, water, noise, and light pollution are serious problems for the National Park Service. Pollution does not recognize arbitrary boundaries set by humans. Humans can, however, take steps to reduce or get rid of the pollution source.

When it comes to pollution, the national parks face threats from outside as well as inside their borders. For example, air pollution from industrialized areas can be carried long distances with prevailing wind currents. Because of prevailing winds on the East coast, Cape Cod

75

National Seashore has some of the highest ozone concentrations of any unit in the National Park Service system. (Ozone is a form of oxygen that is a major type of air pollution.) For Cape Cod, the major pollutants are vehicle emissions.[1]

Glacier National Park in Montana is receiving pollutants from as far away as Asia.[2] In addition, Glacier is affected by another product of pollution: global warming. The park's glacier-covered areas have shrunk by 73 percent from 1850 to 1993. Scientists predict that all the glaciers in the park will be gone by 2030.[3]

The Kyoto Protocol is one international proposal that addresses global warming and pollutants that move between countries (among other topics). However, the protocol must be approved by fifty-five countries that represent altogether 55 percent of the emissions. Without the acceptance of the agreement by Japan, Russia, or the United States, the protocol could not be implemented. Japan ratified the Kyoto Protocol in 2002; Russia announced its intention to ratify in 2003. So far, the United States has rejected the protocol as being bad for the U.S. economy.[4]

Air Pollution

Pollution sources on the industrialized East Coast of the United States damage both animal and plant life in many parks. The U.S. Environmental Protection Agency has estimated that mercury contamination from coal-fired power plants can travel up to six hundred miles.[5] Coal-fired power plants in northern

Mexico generate sulfur dioxide, which contributes to acid rain and decreases visibility. Although the power plants are in compliance with Mexico's environmental laws, the Mexican laws are not as stringent as those of the United States. National Park Service and U.S. Environmental Protection Agency scientists have estimated that the plants account for a 60 percent loss in visibility at Big Bend National Park in Texas. Even though Big Bend is one of the least visited parks in the system, it is one of the most polluted. The National Parks Conservation Association named Big Bend one of the ten most threatened national parks in the country.[6] "Big Bend is not on the way to anywhere else," says Superintendent Frank J. Deckert. "Visitors have to make a special effort to reach the park as it is located in the most remote, least populated area of the continental United States. Just as an example, it is one of the few places left in the country where there is no cell phone service." Air quality (as well as water quality and quantity) are big issues for Big Bend.[7]

Air pollution causes damage to the vegetation, breathing difficulties for humans and other animals, and loss of visibility of scenic vistas. Air pollution also causes something else: water pollution. Air pollution gets into the water cycle and releases acid rain. Some of the streams in the Great Smoky Mountains National Park have lost their fish because of the acidified water from acid rain.

The Blue Ridge Mountains and the Great Smoky Mountains, both part of the southern Appalachian chain, were named for their smoky or blue haze. This effect is caused naturally by the evapotranspiration of the deciduous trees, such as maples and oaks. This is the process through which the trees produce water droplets, which make the sun's light appear to be blue. This gives mountain ranges a color that can be described as blue, smoky, or even majestically purple. However, man-made pollution has added to this haze. The result is a thicker haze that is even brown, instead of purple or blue. This smog then cuts down on visibility, which is important for looking out of the park and into the park.

The Park Service estimates that the visibility at Shenandoah National Park, just north of the Smokies, declined 60 percent between 1948 and 1983. However, perhaps thanks to the most recent amendments to the Clean Air Act (1990), visibility has started to increase at Shenandoah. Between 1991 and 1996, the proportion of summer days with good visibility increased from 16 percent to 31 percent.[8] That means that on one out of about every three summer days, a visitor stopping at an overlook might be able to see over thirty miles away. However, according to a February 27, 2002, briefing statement, "visibility has been reduced from an estimated natural visual range of about 90 miles to an annual average visual range of less than 20 miles and is often lower in the summer."[9] Visitors to Shenandoah often complain about the lack of visibility.

"Smog" is a term originally created by combining the words "smoke" and "fog." It is made up of a variety of pollutants, especially ozone. Smog is often worse farther away from the source of the pollution than near the source. This is because smog is made worse by the chemical reactions that occur between pollutants and sunlight while the wind carries them away from the pollution source.[10] Because of this, our remote national parks have registered higher concentrations of pollutants than some of the industrialized areas. For example, Acadia National Park in Maine was the first place in the country to have an ozone violation, on May 1, 1998. Acadia had higher levels of ozone than the cities of Boston and Philadelphia.[11]

Under the Clean Air Act, forty-nine national parks have been declared Class I wilderness areas.[12] A Class I area is any national park that is bigger than six thousand acres that was established before August 7, 1977. (National wilderness areas have to be over five thousand acres.)[13] Cape Cod National Seashore is a Class II area. This means that the Commonwealth of Massachusetts may permit additional air pollution if national air quality standards are not exceeded and if any increase over the "baseline" amount of pollution is within the allowable range.[14] The Clean Air Act calls for preventing any future man-made impairments on visibility and remedying existing ones.

Water Pollution

Water is all around us. In the national parks, there is water in the lakes, marshes, and streams. It is in the rain. Unseen, underground, there are rivers and aquifers. (Aquifers are underground layers of permeable rock, gravel, or sand that hold water.) All these bodies of water are at risk of being polluted.

Quality and quantity of water are huge issues for Everglades National Park and Big Cypress National Preserve in Florida. They are bordered by growing cities whose actions constantly affect the quality and quantity of water in the park. "As to the larger ecosystem issues, including the disruptions to timing, distribution, quantity and quality of water deliveries, this has been and remains the most significant threat to the park," says Superintendent Maureen Finnerty.[15]

In certain locations, the Park Service has signed contracts with local governments for obtaining water for preserving and maintaining the site. Most of the time, the contract is thought of in terms of how much the park needs to get from the municipality. By public law, the Everglades should receive 315,000 acre feet of water each year from the Central and Southern Florida Project. (An acre foot is defined as one foot of water over one acre of land.) It is often a fight to get enough water for the park. Sometimes, however, the municipality ends up wanting to give the park more than what is in the contract. In the winter of 1983–1984, excess water was dumped in the park, which caused severe environmental damage.[16] Although this "bonus" might seem like a good idea, it was not. It amounted to flooding the park, at great risk to its ecosystems. The diversions of water have resulted in loss of birds. Of the bird populations that were in the park when it was established in 1947, less than 10 percent have survived.[17]

Water issues, both of quality and quantity, affect floodplains, wetlands, and watersheds. Floodplains are areas along rivers that are routinely flooded with high water, such as after torrential rains or after spring thaws of snow. The Park Service tries to preserve the floodplains while still keeping any damage to a minimum. Watersheds are areas over which water runs on its way to streams and rivers. Wetlands are areas like marshes and swamps where water naturally collects and pools. The National Park Service, like other federal agencies, has a policy that there should be no net loss of wetlands, because they attract animals and plants specific to such an environment. In fact, where wetlands are unavoidably damaged, the Park Service will restore other wetlands to make up for the loss. For each acre destroyed, the NPS must restore an acre.[18]

One other water issue that relates to quantity, rather than water quality, is the existence of dams. Today, the Park Service will not construct any dams on national park lands.[19] The National Park Service also reevaluates any existing dams to make sure that they are crucial to the surrounding community. The importance of an existing dam to the community is a combination of economic, recreational, and water supply considerations. Man-made dams cause natural features to be flooded and become inaccessible. They also affect the natural stream flow and thereby impair it. Dams can also pose a danger if the dam becomes damaged. It is therefore the goal of the NPS to "minimize human disturbance to the natural upland processes that deliver water, sediment, and woody debris to streams."[20]

Soundscapes and Noise Pollution

Sound is defined as vibrations disturbing the membranes of an ear. This stimulus leads to hearing. So this answers an old riddle: If a tree falls in the forest and no one, not even an animal, is there to hear it, it does *not* make a sound. (This is, of course, impossible.) Sound is a physical process or effect. It is measured with acoustic instruments and reported in decibels.

Noise, on the other hand, is a psychological effect. It is sound that is not welcome or is annoying or even harmful. It relates to how people feel about it. Such an effect is hard to measure.[21] So the challenge in preserving natural soundscapes lies in determining what types of sound should be allowed to intrude. Are human-caused sounds appropriate in national parks? It would be unreasonable, most people would agree, to forbid *any* human sound. Then the discussion becomes one of determining how loud, how frequent, and how much human-caused sound should be permitted.

Some scientists have studied the effects of noise on visitors' experiences in national parks. To measure the effects of noise, the researchers have to physically measure the sound and then ask people how they feel about the noise. Unfortunately, by asking someone this question, a scientist then affects the outcome. A visitor might not have consciously noticed a certain sound until someone mentions it. Then it drives him or her crazy!

Sounds of nature tend to be more accepted by the average park visitor. That is, after all, part of the park experience. Other sounds, however, can intrude upon and even ruin the quality of a visit. These sounds might be from cars or snowmobiles in the park, trucks on a highway outside the park, helicopters flying over the park, water purification systems run by the park employees, or other sources. People traveling alone or in small groups can even be annoyed by the sounds made by large groups of other visitors.

Studies conducted by the Park Service, the U.S. Forest Service, and others have shown that there are three major ways to deal with noise pollution. One method is to reduce or eliminate the noise itself. Another method is to produce other sounds to mask or cover the noise. (This is called "white noise.") A third method is to provide a stimulus or activity that makes the visitor less likely to notice the noise in the first place.[22]

Visitors to the Grand Canyon National Park are often bothered by the helicopters and small planes that fly over the park to give tourists a view of the canyon—often called "flightseeing" tours. In 2000, the Federal Aviation Administration (FAA) limited the number of flights over the Grand Canyon to ninety thousand per year. Even at that, many operators of aircraft that offer tours over the Grand Canyon have complained. The tour operators feel that the restriction is forcing them out of business. Flights are also an issue for Glacier (Montana), Zion, Bryce Canyon, Arches, and Canyonlands (Utah), and Hawaii Volcanoes National Parks.[23] Denali National Park and Preserve in Alaska also has to contend with people landing airplanes in the park, not just flying over. (Parts of Denali are accessible only by plane or dogsled.) At first it may seem obvious that aircraft noise is a bad addition to the Grand Canyon experience. However, just as with other battles over visitor activities, not all visitors choose to enjoy a park in the same way. There is no clear winner—no solution will make everyone happy.

Who is to say how each person should enjoy a park? Some people argue that visitors' enjoyment should not affect those around them. Everyone is entitled to visit and enjoy the national parks. However, the noise made by a cross-country skier cannot disturb a person on a snowmobile. A snowmobile is surely going to disturb—and perhaps endanger—a skier. Its noise can travel up to ten miles on either side, penetrating deep into the wilderness. We cannot do everything we want all the time, especially if it infringes on the rights of others. As Devereux Butcher (former executive director of the National Parks Association) said:

> We all have the same right to come into the parks for the delight and spiritual uplift they have been established to provide; but no one has the right or special privilege to roar through the parks, battering vegetation, disturbing wildlife and other visitors.[24]

In some cases, snowmobiles are the preferred means of transportation. For example, in Alaska's Denali National Park and Preserve, snowmobiles are needed because the ranger stations are so spread out. Also, because of 1980's Alaska National Interest Land Conservation Act, Denali now has 2 million acres where snowmobiles have been allowed for a long time. When that land was added to the park, the NPS worked out agreements with the surrounding communities that would allow them to continue to

Human visitors can enjoy the national parks in many different ways. But even picture-taking can cause a problem if it disturbs animals or blocks traffic.

use their snowmobiles on what was now Park Service land.

Noise intrusion is sometimes unavoidable. The parks that are located in or near major cities cannot shut off the cars or factories. But national park visitors can play a part in reducing noise pollution. When people visit national parks, they should remember that they are visitors. This place is some other creatures' home, which should be treated with respect. In turn, they will enjoy their park experience more.

Other Resources to Protect From Human Pollution

Besides air, water, and soundscapes, there are other natural conditions where humans have interfered. The Park Service goal is always to prevent any future damage and repair any current damage. For example, artificial light from human activities and facilities can confuse little turtle hatchlings as they try to find their way to the sea. Lights visible in deep caves can affect the mating of animals that are used to living in total darkness. Therefore, the Park Service discourages the use of artificial light. Where absolutely necessary for visitor safety, such artificial light is supposed to be shielded or covered so it has the smallest effect on the natural conditions.

Another type of human-caused pollution is from chemicals or odors. Many animals use smell to distinguish their mating, migration, and social structure patterns. Flowers use scent to attract certain types of bees and insects to cross-pollinate the flower. Even rocks and soils give off certain smells that can tell fish where they need to lay their eggs. Any type of smells created by humans that interfere with these natural processes should be avoided.

The many ways that we are polluting our national parks could fill a book. One important pollutant is from accidental spills, especially in coastal and river parks. Spills have lasting impacts on park coastal resources. For example, Padre Island National Seashore in Texas has suffered oil spills from internal oil and gas production facilities that have contaminated park groundwater and wetlands. A pipeline spill at Georgia's Chickamauga and Chattanooga National Military Park contaminated a cave system.[25] In Alaska, Katmai National Park and Preserve shoreline resources were devastated by the 1989 *Exxon Valdez* oil spill. Between thirty-five hundred and fifty-five hundred sea otters were killed. Harlequin ducks in the Prince William Sound failed to reproduce as a result of the spill. Harbor seals suffered nervous system injuries. These are just a few examples of the injury to wildlife.[26]

Humans are the cause of most pollution. Government can pass laws and regulate the amount of pollution. However, it is also up to all individuals to have as little impact on natural resources as possible.

6

Culture Clash

Should the National Park Service always have the right to protect and preserve our history? The answer might seem to be an obvious "yes," but it is not as easy as that. Our history includes cultures with many different traditions from those of mainstream America. Unfortunately, members of mainstream American society have not always given the sites of other cultures the respect they would want for their own religious sites and personal effects. And the NPS has reflected this. Grave sites were dug up and artifacts were removed for study. Even human

88

remains were moved. The accepted way to handle such archaeological sites in the past was to dig them up and display what was found in museums. However, we have come to understand in more recent years that this is disrespectful to peoples and cultures. The Park Service then has to balance the sincere need to study and learn about ancient peoples with the genuine need to respect their sacred ground.

In 1906, President Theodore Roosevelt signed the American Antiquities Act. This was in direct response to a desire to protect the Native American Indian grave sites and other artifacts in the Southwest. (Ironically, though, it was first used to protect a geological feature—Devils Tower, in Wyoming.) When it comes to protecting our culture, there are many laws and rules that govern the national parks' responsibility.

American Indians

Within the National Park Service system, there are areas that are classified as national parks but are not owned by the United States government. Instead, they are owned by tribal governments. For example, Pipe Spring National Monument is in the middle of the Kaibab Paiute Reservation; Kaibab Paiute Indians run the visitor center and campground.[1] Some natural and cultural resources are of significance to American Indian groups or other traditionally associated peoples. For example, for thousands of years, the Chacoan people have conducted ceremonial events according to the stars. Because of this, in 1993, the Chaco Culture National Historical Park declared the night sky to be a critical resource that must be protected. Since then, all park lighting has been changed to reduce pollution from artificial light sources.[2] The area is considered sacred by the Pueblo of New Mexico, the Hopi of Arizona, and the Navajo of the Southwest.

Members of these groups differ from other park visitors because the resources of the park have a special significance to them. The land is tied to the group's purpose and development as a people. The site might have religious significance or represent

This picture, taken at Chaco Canyon, New Mexico, in 1966, shows an ancient Indian site that is being excavated by archaeologists. Called a kiva, the structure was used in Pueblo Indian ceremonies.

typical migration routes or include an area that has been farmed or hunted for generations. The significance to the tribe or group is not related to the fact that the land is a national park. When the significance to the tribe or group is expression of religion, the NPS is especially committed to helping the group. To interfere with the practice of their religion would deprive members of the group of their First and Fourteenth Amendment rights under the U.S. Constitution.

When members of these associated peoples visit the park to conduct their traditional activities, they are not charged an entrance fee. Park Service personnel are also instructed not to call attention to the activities or to announce their presence to other park visitors. This consideration is to preserve the dignity and privacy of people involved in ceremonial activities.

Whenever possible, the Park Service discusses any discovered artifacts and sites with current members of the culture group. Their wishes are then given preference. In dealing with American Indian peoples, the Park Service recognizes many tribes that other federal agencies have not. Tribes or cultural groups can first be recognized by federal or state agencies. They are also recognized by the Park Service if they define themselves as a tribe and share a language, family structure, political system, or other similar features.[3]

According to its management policies, the National Park Service considers a tribe to be associated with a park if the group has been involved with the community or park for at least two generations (about forty years), the tie between the group and the land began before the national park was established, and the group thinks of the park and its resources as being key to its identity as a cultural group.[4]

In 1990, Congress directed the National Park Service to study the needs of American Indian tribes in preserving their properties and cultural traditions. Ever since the first Europeans set foot on this continent, native peoples' cultures have been damaged. Lands were taken away, tribes were wiped out, and languages were lost. Finally, in the late twentieth century, the American Indian people began to "gain ground." One program that has helped this progress is the National Park Service's Tribal Preservation Program. This program is a partnership between the Park Service, Indian tribes, native Hawaiians, Alaska Native Groups, and other organizations dedicated to preserving the traditions of Native American peoples. The Tribal Preservation Program has assisted twenty-seven tribes in assuming formal preservation responsibilities (according to the National Historic Preservation Act). The program has also directly helped more than two hundred tribes receive $21.9 million in grant funds. The money is used to study and protect historical sites, among many other important activities.[5]

Burial Sites

The national park lands contain many known and unknown graves and burial sites. The Park Service tries to find, document, and protect as many of these prehistoric and historic sites as possible. When new facilities are being constructed, the Park Service makes every effort to leave any grave sites undisturbed. In case remains of American Indians are disturbed or accidentally removed, the National Park Service works with members of the appropriate Native American group or tribe. The remains can then be reburied in the same park from which they were removed.

No human remains or photographs of human remains can be exhibited. With permission of the appropriate cultural group (members of the tribe affected, if the tribe still exists), drawings or casts of the remains are allowed. The overall goal is to treat people with dignity and according to the wishes of their descendants. As stated in the NPS management policies, "The preservation of cultural resources in their existing states will always receive first consideration."[6]

Another situation that arises with ancestors is family cemeteries. There are fifteen national cemeteries and countless family cemeteries on Park Service lands. The National Park Service manages all national cemeteries in national parks as historically significant resources. People can be buried in these national cemeteries (usually if they served in the military) until the cemetery has been filled. The cemetery cannot be expanded because that would impair or intrude upon the existing historical nature of the cemetery itself.[7]

National Park Service policy states that family

members can still be buried in the family cemeteries until there is no more space available. The family cemeteries are taken care of by the families. (For this they are allowed to enter the park without paying, because their purpose is not to visit the park.) The superintendent of the park keeps a record of who is buried where.

How did family cemeteries end up in the middle of a national park? They certainly did not start out that way. The cemeteries were there long before the park was established. Some parks are authorized by Congress to allow historical activities to continue on

Many people do not know that some national parks contain family cemeteries. This cemetery is located in Cades Cove, Great Smoky Mountains National Park. The latest marker is dated 1996.

the lands acquired. Some parks allow ranching, farming, or other minimal uses that have historically been practiced. American Indian groups who have used part of a park over generations are allowed to continue that practice for traditional or religious purposes.

From Private Property to National Park

Some of the property that became national parks had been in one family for generations. In most cases, the land was donated to the federal government. However, in some instances, the government obtained plots of land through more aggressive means. Sometimes safety dictates the need for the Park Service to acquire the land. Wherever possible, the Park Service makes every reasonable effort to obtain the land through agreement on a purchase price. However, if the owner and Park Service cannot come to agreement, then the government can take additional steps to get the land.

One method is to condemn the property and then claim it. This is almost always the last resort. One example of when this authority might be used is if park resources are threatened by something happening outside the park. With an authority called "eminent domain," the government is able to buy property from private citizens—even if they do not want to sell. In the case of pollution, sometimes the threat is far from the park. In this case, park officials work with area agencies to find a solution to the problem.

The government is required to pay a fair market price. However, if a family has lived on a piece of land for generations and does not want to sell, no price will seem fair to them. This can be the start of a bad relationship. The Skyline Drive and Shenandoah National Park, for example, were established in the 1920s. Feelings against the government were so strong even into the 1970s that new employees were told to be careful about going down into the hollows (or "hollers") in uniform.

Remembering American History

Some national parks were established to commemorate sad events in American history. Our national park system is unique in the world for its recognition of the good and bad parts of America's history.

On December 7, 1941, Japanese planes attacked Pearl Harbor, a U.S. naval station in Hawaii. (At the time of the attack, Hawaii was not yet a state, and the United States was not yet at war with Japan.) Many ships were sunk, including the U.S.S. *Arizona*, which is now a national monument.

Altogether, about twenty-four hundred American sailors, soldiers, and civilians who were in ships and on land were killed. About twelve hundred were wounded. The attack crippled the U.S. Navy's Pacific fleet and propelled the United States into World War II.

On February 19, 1942, President Franklin D. Roosevelt signed an executive order to relocate 110,000 people of Japanese descent. Their property was taken away from them and they were forced into internment camps, where they lived in barracks. Many, if not all, of these Americans did not identify with Japan. Many were native-born or naturalized American citizens. Some of them had sons and husbands who were fighting in the U.S. armed forces. It was a low point in American history.

Manzanar National Historic Site is a five hundred–acre site in the Owens Valley of eastern California. It is the site of one of the ten interment camps, the Manzanar War Relocation Center, which operated from 1942 to 1945. Manzanar held ten thousand people captive at its peak (or worst) point. There were 576 one-story buildings that were twenty feet wide and one hundred feet long, divided into thirty-six blocks. Each family was put into a space in these barracks that was about twenty feet square.[8]

In 1988, President Ronald Reagan signed legislation to offer an apology and payment to each family affected by the internment. Some people think internment was the right thing to do and do not approve of the apology, the restitution payment, or the national historic site. However, those who established the site believe it is important to remember such events of the past so that they might not be repeated.

Another time in our history where the people were divided over what we believed was right was during the Korean War, in which Americans fought from 1950 to 1953. Over 55,000 Americans died in the war; 103,000 were wounded and 8,000 were missing in action. However, some Korean War veterans were disappointed that it took the United States all the way to 1995 to dedicate a memorial to honor the veterans. The Korean War Veterans Memorial, authorized in 1986 by Congress, occupies two acres near the Lincoln Memorial in Washington, D.C. The memorial consists of nineteen seven-foot statues representing Americans of a variety of descents: European, African, Hispanic, Asian, and American Indian. The statues also represent different branches of the armed forces as follows: fourteen members of the Army, three Marines, one Navy medic, and one Air Force observer. The figures wear

During World War II, thousands of Japanese Americans were forced into internment camps. Here, people at Manzanar War Relocation Center in California walk to their barracks after church. Today Manzanar is a national historic site.

rain gear to show the conditions under which these men and women served.[9]

The Vietnam Veterans Memorial is a two-acre site, located northeast of the Lincoln Memorial. This memorial, dedicated in 1982, honors those who fought in Vietnam from 1963 to 1972. Two walls of polished black granite nearly 250 feet long meet at a 125-degree angle, like a black V cut into the land behind them. The walls are carved with the 58,235 names of those who died as a result of wounds incurred in the war or were missing in action. The design chosen was a surprise to many. The designer, Maya Ying Lin, was a twenty-one-year-old female Asian-American architecture student. Despite the initial feelings of surprise, Lin's creation has provided much needed healing for the people who fought in this controversial war as well as their family and friends.

7

Safety and the Future

The future of the national parks is currently under debate. Some people would like to preserve the parks as they are. Others see the parks as a rich source of untapped resources.

This dispute has a long history. In 1948, the U. S. Army Corps of Engineers proposed a power dam on the north fork of the Flathead River.[1] A dam was also proposed on the Rio Grande River, which would impair Big Bend National Park.[2] In Glacier Bay National Park in Alaska, Congress legalized mining from 1938 to 1950. Finally, even though new gold

100

deposits were found, Congress outlawed mining once and for all.[3]

For over 130 years, our parks have struggled with many issues from inside and outside their borders. The first years of the twenty-first century have brought new threats to light: threats from outside the country's borders. In 1999 a study was conducted by a panel to determine the safety of many public facilities, partially in response to the 1995 bombing of the Murrah Federal Building in Oklahoma City, Oklahoma. The panel was commissioned by the Pentagon. In its report, the panel predicted that the coming years would be marked by attacks on private citizens where they worked, lived, played, and relaxed. The report was eerily on target: "Americans will become increasingly vulnerable to hostile attack on our homeland, and our military superiority will not entirely protect us."[4]

On September 11, 2001, the World Trade Center Towers in New York City and the Pentagon in Washington, D.C., were attacked by three airliners that had been hijacked by terrorists. A fourth plane crashed in a field in Pennsylvania after its passengers apparently overcame the hijackers. It is not known if the White House was the intended target of the fourth plane, but no Park Service facilities were directly attacked. However, National Park Service sites were affected. All NPS sites were closed immediately after it became obvious that the attacks were not accidents.

The Federal Hall National Memorial stands near the World Trade Center. It is the site where George

Washington took the oath of office to become the first president of the United States. Before the attacks on September 11, the aging building was beginning to show signs of wear. A study was in progress to see what should be done and how to pay for any repairs. Now the repairs needed are much more extensive and will be much more expensive.

Another site that was affected by the attacks was the Statue of Liberty National Monument. While under attack, the United States closed its borders. Even into 2003, the Statue of Liberty itself was still closed to all visitors.

All 450 National Park Service employees in New York Harbor assisted in the search-and-rescue operations. Park Service employees from the Statue of Liberty and Ellis Island also ran boats for evacuating victims to bypass the congested streets that could not hold any more traffic. Park Service personnel also worked overtime at Gateway National Recreation Area to help contain the crowds who had gathered to stare at the incomplete New York skyline.[5] Jill Hawk, the chief ranger of Mount Rainier National Park, went to New York City to be on a Critical Incident Stress Management Team, counseling and supporting NPS employees.[6]

The Role of the Park Ranger

In people's imaginations, rangers seem to symbolize the parks themselves: wholesome, good, and pure, almost like the romanticized cowboys of the old West. But like the parks themselves, park rangers are also refining their roles and seeking new ways to provide services to the public. So what do park rangers do? Who are they?

Not all park rangers do the same type of work. Some focus on law enforcement, carry a gun, and can even issue tickets and arrest people. Many rangers are also trained as firefighters, emergency medical technicians, and paramedics.

National Park Service employees perform many different kinds of jobs—as naturalists, interpreters, firefighters, paramedics, and more. This park ranger works on the National Mall in Washington, D.C.

Some park rangers are naturalists or interpreters. They describe the natural and cultural resources to visitors. The naturalists and interpreters combine their expertise with sharp people skills to make their knowledge accessible to all visitors. The interpreters educate and entertain and help the visitor gain a sense of personal ownership of the national park. Naturalists can be found at visitor centers and conducting evening programs at campgrounds.

As the types of activities and visitor expectations change, the role of the ranger has changed, too. Park Service employees are also now being trained to handle hazardous materials, to find and capture terrorists, and to conduct search-and-rescue operations. In all activities, visitor safety will take precedence over any other considerations.

Working for the National Park Service

Thirty years ago, there were about six hundred applicants for every job at a national park. The application process was confusing, with a complicated application form. Now, because of the Internet, people who are interested in working for the National Park Service can apply more easily. That means, however, that there are currently more than two thousand applicants for each job. There are about sixteen thousand permanent employees. During the peak seasons (mostly summer and fall), the Park Service adds about six thousand seasonal or temporary employees. And across the whole National

Park Service system there are also ninety thousand volunteers.[7]

Park rangers are not the only kind of Park Service employees. The Park Service also employs fire-fighters; administrative people; maintenance, trade, and craft people; police officers; uniformed guards; biologists; physical scientists; experts in cultural resources; writers; photographers; and many others.

There are many degrees that can lead to a career with the National Park Service. Generally a background in either natural science or social science is good preparation for a naturalist or interpretative position. Protective or ranger positions are filled best by people who have backgrounds or training in public administration, law enforcement, or public safety.

Future of the National Parks

People will always be interested in our country's cultural and natural resources. However, our understanding of how to treat those resources changes. The future of the national parks depends on what the political climate is and how much support Congress gives the National Park Service. The 1980s stand out as a decade marked by increases in visitation along with massive decreases in park funding. As a result, the parks suffered overcrowding, understaffing, deterioration of roads and facilities, and a drop in morale among employees.[8]

In the 2000–2001 Business Plan for Denali National Park and Preserve, Superintendent Stephen

Martin confirmed that this is still the case. "An aging infrastructure, increasing operational costs, and growing visitor numbers threaten to sacrifice the values for which your park was established."[9]

An environmental assessment was conducted in Denali to determine acceptable traffic levels. The study concluded that the park has reached 79 percent of its capacity. "Without additional visitor activities [to spread out the concentration of visitors], the Park Road will reach its maximum carrying capacity by 2005."[10] Trains carry visitors to various stations throughout the park. However, that means that most of the visitors arrive according to the train schedule. Because the Park Road is one of a few ways for visitors to access the park, there is no way to separate the visitors' arrivals and departures from the schedule of the trains.[11]

In October 1991, National Park Service managers met in Vail, Colorado, along with environmentalists, scholars, and other park supporters. The goal was to reach an understanding on the issues facing the Park Service. What was developed has come to be called the "Vail Agenda." The group concluded that there was a "wide and discouraging gap between the service's potential and its current state." The group felt that many decisions in the past had been based on political agendas or hunches, rather than on scientific research. In fact, very few of the highest ranked park managers had (or have) scientific backgrounds.[12]

Douglas Morris, superintendent of Shenandoah National Park, summed it up best after the Vail conference. "The future of the Park Service depends on an engaged public. An engaged public engages elected officials," Morris said. "The threats against parks will never go away. It's not a job you do and it's over."[13]

Each of us can preserve our parks by being respectful visitors. We can also volunteer at the parks or even work for the National Park Service or one of its concessionaires. Issues affecting our national parks affect all of us. We need to be sensitive to these issues and our role in their solution. We cannot take park preservation for granted. It will take more research and an informed and engaged public to ensure that the Park Service meets its mandate of preserving its resources "unimpaired for future generations."

Chapter Notes

Chapter 1. National Parks: Yesterday and Today

1. David Backes, ed., *Sigurd F. Olson, The Meaning of Wilderness: Essential Articles and Speeches* (Minneapolis: University of Minnesota Press, 2001), p. 78.

2. William Booth, "At Yellowstone, The Din of Snowmobiles and Debate," *Washington Post*, February 6, 2003, <http://www.washingtonpost. com> (April 2, 2003); Todd Wilkinson, "Yellowstone Weighs Snowmobile Versus Serenity," *The Christian Science Monitor*, December 6, 1999, <http://csmweb2.emcweb.com/durable/1999/12/ 06/p2s2.htm> (April 2, 2003); J.R. Pegg, "Bush Opens Yellowstone to More Snowmobiles," *Environment News Service*, November 11, 2002, <http://ens-news.com/ens/nov2002/2002-11-13- 10.asp> (April 2, 2003).

3. *Management Policies 2001,* NPS D1416, National Park Service, Washington, D.C., December 2000, p. 1.

4. "National Park Service: Employment Information," March 21, 2002, <http://www.nps. gov/personnel/> (January 14, 2003).

5. *Management Policies 2001*, p. 30.

6. "NPS Planning," January 14, 2003 <http:// planning.nps.gov/default.cfm> (January 14, 2003).

7. "Frequently Asked Questions About the National Park Service," updated July 17, 2001, <http://www.nps.gov/pub_aff/e-mail/faqs.htm> (July 14, 2002).

8. *Management Policies 2001*, p. 10.

9. Ibid.

10. Paul Schullery, *Searching for Yellowstone* (New York: Houghton Mifflin, 1997), pp. 112–115.

11. Ibid., pp. 111 and 115.

12. "National Park Service History: History of the National Park Service, A Brief History," n.d., <http://www.cr.nps.gov/history/hisnps/NPSHistory/npshisto.htm> (January 14, 2003).

13. Schullery, p. 128.

14. *Management Policies 2001*, p. 11.

15. "Mission 66: Quarry Visitor Center, Dinosaur National Monument, Jensen, Utah," October 7, 2002, <http://www.cr.nps.gov/history/online_books/allaback/vc1.htm> (January 22, 2003).

16. Devereux Butcher, *Exploring Our National Parks and Monuments*, Revised Eighth Edition (Boston: Harvard Common Press, 1986), p. 360.

17. "Mission 66 and the Environmental Era, 1952 to 1970," *The National Parks: Shaping the System*, October 7, 2002, <http://www.cr.nps.gov/history/online_books/mackintosh1/sts2d.htm> (May 15, 2003); and "Rounding Out the System," October 7, 2002, <http://www.cr.nps.gov/history/online_books/mackintosh/sts2e.htm> (May 15, 2003).

18. "The Problem of Winter Use," in *Mount Rainier Administrative History, Part Five: Contentious Years, 1945–1965*, July 24, 2000, <http://www.nps.gov/mora/adhi/adhi14.htm> (January 17, 2003).

19. "Organic Act and Stewardship of Resources," August 19, 2002, <http://www2.nature.nps.gov/ardnew/policy/npsoasteward.htm> (January 17, 2003).

20. Ibid.

21. *Thomas* v. *Reagan*, USDC Cr. No. 84–3552, n.d., <http://prop1.org/legal/843532/870306a1.htm> (May 16, 2003).

22. "National Park Service History: Administrative Histories," September 6, 2001, <http://www.cr.nps.gov/history/hisnps/NPSHistory/antiq.htm> (January 14, 2003).

23. Committee on Resources, Subcommittee on National Parks and Public Lands, Witness Statement, March 14, 2000, <http://resourcescommittee.house.gov/106cong/parks/00mar14/emmons_hr3084.htm> (February 1, 2002).

24. Bob Ribokas, "Supai and the Havasupai Reservation," n.d., <http://www.kaibab.org/supai/gc_supai.htm> (July 14, 2002).

25. Butcher, p. 78.

26. *Management Policies 2001*, p. 130.

27. Ibid., p. 89.

28. Butcher, p. 90.

29. "Antiquities Act of 1906," n.d., <http://www.cr.nps.gov/history/hisnps/NPSHistory/antiq.htm> (January 14, 2003).

30. Butcher, p. 90.

31. Backes, pp. xiv–xvii.

32. Russell D. Butcher, *Exploring Our National Historic Parks and Sites* (Niwot, Colo.: Roberts Rinehart Publishers in cooperation with the National Parks and Conservation Association, 1997), p. 506.

33. Max King, "Glen Canyon—The Place No One Knew," July 21, 2001, <http://www.nps.gov/glca/history.htm> (January 17, 2003).

Chapter 2. Fire!

1. Personal experience of the author, circa 1979.

2. Steve Nix, "Five Fire Disasters—The Final Reports," May 21, 2000, <http://forestry.about.com/library/weekly/aa052100.htm> (June 12, 2002).

3. Steve Nix, "Smokey Bear—A 55 Year [sic] Career," September 13, 1998, <http://forestry.about.com/library/weekly/aa091398.htm> (June 11, 2002).

4. "Only You Can Prevent Wildfires!" The Ad Councii, the National Association of State Foresters and the United States Forest Service, news release, April 23, 2001, <http://forestry.about.com/library/weekly/aa043001a. htm > (June 11, 2002).

5. "Fire Management," Shenandoah NP: Shenandoah Stories, November 24, 1999, <http://www.nps.gov/shen/3a7.htm> (May 16, 2003).

6. "Develop or Update a Wildlife Response Plan" (draft), *The Fire Management Process*, October 9, 1999, <http://tncfire.org/manual/wildfire.htm> (June 12, 2002).

7. "Shenandoah: Fire Management," November 24, 1999, <http://www.nps.gov/shen/3a7.htm> (June 13, 2002).

8. "Worst U.S. Forest Fires," n.d., <http://www.infoplease.com/ipa/AO778688.html> (June 12, 2002).

9. Bruce T. Gourley, "Yellowstone: The Second Century," updated August 30, 2000, <http://www.yellowstone.net/history.htm> (June 12, 2002).

10. "Wildland Fire," October 3, 2001, <http://www.nps.gov/yell/nature/fire> (June 12, 2002).

11. Nix, "Five Fire Disasters—The Final Reports."

12. Lary M. Dilsaver, ed., *America's National Park System: The Critical Documents*, Chapter 8: "A System Threatened, 1981–1992," updated October 25, 2000, <http://www.cr.nps.gov/history/online_books/anps/anps_8.htm> (November 20, 2001).

13. "Wildfire," updated 2001, <http://www.redcross.org/services/disaster/keepsafe/ready-wildfire.html> (June 12, 2002)

14. "Only You Can Prevent Wildfires!"

Chapter 3. Flora and Fauna

1. Gary Paulsen, *Guts: The True Stories Behind* Hatchet *and the Brian Books* (New York: Delacorte Press, 2001), p. 55.

2. "An Ounce of Prevention," n.d., <http://www.nps.gov/brca/naprevention.htm> (January 17, 2003).

3. *Management Policies 2001*, NPS D1416, National Park Service, Washington, D.C., December 2000, p. 38.

4. Bob Miller, "Smokies Announces Experimental Brook Trout Fishery Project," press release, May 29, 2002, <http://www.nps.gov/grsm/gsmsite/troutPR.htm> (July 15, 2002).

5. *Management Policies 2001*, p. 34.

6. "Cades Cove Tour," Great Smoky Mountains Natural History Association brochure, 1999, p. 22.

7. Bob Miller, "New Forest Insect Pest Discovered in Smokies," press release, May 16, 2002, <http://www.nps.gov/grsm/gsmsite/hemlockadelgidrel.htm> (July 15, 2002).

8. Personal interview with Bob Miller, Great Smoky Mountains National Park information specialist, February 22, 2002.

9. Rich Evans, "Delaware Water Gap National Recreation Area Hemlock Woolly Adelgid Biocontrol Beetle Release," press release, June 12, 2000, <http://www.nps.gov/dewa/pressea/hwa2.html> (July 15, 2002).

10. "Cades Cove Tour," p. 28.

11. Blair Howard, *Adventure Guide to the Great Smoky Mountains* (Edison, N.J.: Hunter Publishing, Inc., 2001), p. 8.

12. Ibid., p. 100.

13. Personal interview with Charlie Jacobi, resource specialist, Acadia National Park, March 14, 2002.

14. *Management Policies 2001*, p. 37.

15. Paul Schullery, *Searching for Yellowstone* (New York: Houghton Mifflin, 1997), p. 79.

16. Ibid., p. 77.

17. Ibid., p. 126.

18. Ibid., pp. 47–48.

19. Letter to the author from John J. Donahue, superintendent of Big Cypress National Preserve, May 3, 2002.

20. "All Things Considered," National Public Radio, January 8, 2003.

21. "Bighorn Sheep," Utah Division of Wildlife Resources, Wildlife Notebook Series No. 16, May

2000, <http://www.wildlife.utah.gov/publications/pdf/bighorntwo.pdf> (January 13, 2003).

22. "To Re-establish an Extirpated Species," February 1, 2000, <http://www.cr.nps.gov/history/online_books/fauna1/fauna3-1.htm> (January 19, 2003).

23. "Capitol Reef—Unfunded Research Needs," Catalog of National Park Service Research Needs, Colorado Plateau Cooperative Ecosystem Studies Unit, July 9, 2002, <http://cpcesu.nau.edu/pmis/CARE4pmis1.htm> (January 19, 2003).

24. "Restored Species," December 18, 1997, <http://www.nature.nps.gov/wv/ressp.htm> (January 19, 2003).

Chapter 4. Visitors and Carrying Capacity

1. David Backes, ed., *Sigurd F. Olson, The Meaning of Wilderness: Essential Articles and Speeches* (Minneapolis: University of Minnesota Press, 2001), p. 44.

2. Paul Schullery, *Searching for Yellowstone* (New York: Houghton Mifflin, 1997), p. 5.

3. *Management Policies 2001*, NPS D1416, National Park Service, Washington, D.C., December 2000, p. 81.

4. Ibid., p. 53.

5. E-mail to the author from Marsha L. Karle, Chief, Public Affairs, Yellowstone National Park, March 13, 2002.

6. Backes, p. 148.

7. E-mail to author from Charlie Jacobi, resource specialist at Acadia National Park, March 4, 2002.

8. "Principles of Leave No Trace," n.d., <http://www.lnt.org/welcome.html> (March 12, 2002).

9. Jacobi.

10. "Cades Cove Tour," Great Smoky Mountains Natural History Association brochure, 1999, pp. 19 and 23.

11. Committee on Resources, Subcommittee on National Parks & Public Lands, Witness Statement, July 20, 2000, <http://resourcescommittee.house. gov/106cong/parks/00jul20/galvin.htm> (February 1, 2002).

12. Thomas C. Jester and Sharon C. Park, AIA, "Making Historic Properties Accessible," *Preservation Briefs: No. 32*, September 1993, <http://www2.cr.nps.gov/TPS/briefs/brief32. htm> (January 21, 2003).

13. *Management Policies 2001*, p. 53.

14. Schullery, p. 90.

15. Ibid., p. 92.

16. Ibid., pp. 92–94.

17. "Concessions," *North Cascades National Park: Contested Terrain: An Administrative History* (Chapter 4), April 14, 1999, <http://www.nps. gov/noca/adhi-4.htm>, (January 21, 2003).

18. *Management Policies 2001*, p. 100.

19. Committee on Resources, Subcommittee on National Parks & Public Lands, Witness Statement, July 20, 2000, <http://resourcescommittee. house.gov/106cong/parks/00jul20/galvin.htm> (February 1, 2002).

20. Ibid.

21. "Guide's Guide to National Parks," n.d., <http://www.nps.gov/tourism/New_Folder/ sp19521gp.html> (January 21, 2003).

22. E-mail to the author from Dave Dahlen, Chief of Interpretation, Glacier National Park, May 12, 2002.

Chapter 5. Fighting Pollution

1. *Forging a Collaborative Future: General Management Plan*, Cape Cod National Seashore, Barnstable County, Massachusetts, July 7, 1998, p. 27.

2. "Air Toxics," June 3, 2002, <http://www.aqd.nps.gov/ard/aqmon/air_toxics/> (January 19, 2003).

3. "Glacier National Park," *Across the Nation*, National Parks Conservation Association, n.d., <http://www.npca.org/across_the_nation/vis...perience/code_red/fact_sheets/glacier.asp> (January 19, 2003).

4. Matthew Taylor, "Climate Change in the Asia-Pacific Region: Opportunity and Crisis," Fall 2001, <http://www.mcpa.org/pubs_videos/pub_pdfs/taylor.pdf> (January 19, 2003).

5. "Air Pollution in our National Parks—1999," *Izaak Walton League Reports*, n.d., <http://www.iwla.org/reports/parktext.html> (July 15, 2002).

6. "Big Bend National Park Carbon I and II Power Plants Fact Sheet," National Park Service, February 1995.

7. Letter to the author from Frank J. Deckert, superintendent of Big Bend National Park, March 5, 2002.

8. "Air Quality and Air Pollution Impacts, Shenandoah National Park," Briefing Statement, National Park Service, February 27, 2002.

9. Ibid.

10. "The Plain English Guide to the Clean Air Act," n.d., <http://www.epa.gov/oar/oaqps/peg_caa/pegcaa10.html> (June 9, 2002).

11. "Air Pollution in Our National Parks—1999."

12. "NPS Text List of Class I Parks," February 22, 1999, <http://www2.nature.nps.gov/ard/parks/parklistc1.html> (February 22, 2002).

13. *Management Policies 2001*, NPS D1416, National Park Service, Washington, D.C., December 2000, p. 41.

14. *Forging a Collaborative Future: General Management Plan*, p. 27.

15. Letter to the author from Maureen Finnerty, superintendent of Everglades National Park and Dry Tortugas National Park, April 26, 2002.

16. Devereux Butcher, *Exploring Our National Parks and Monuments*, Revised Eighth Edition (Boston: The Harvard Common Press, 1986), p. 60.

17. Russell D. Butcher, *National Parks and Conservation Association: Exploring Our National Historical Parks and Sites* (Niwot, Colo.: Roberts Rinehart Publishers, 1997), p. 477.

18. *Management Policies*, pp. 39–40.

19. Ibid., p. 114.

20. Ibid., p. 40.

21. Dr. James Gramann, "The Effect of Mechanical Noise and Natural Sound on Visitor Experiences in Units of the National Park System," *Social Science Research Review*, vol. 1, no. 1, Winter 1999.

22. Ibid.

23. Robert Gehrke, "Court hears argument in lawsuit over Grand Canyon flights," May 10, 2002, <http://www.montanaforum.com/rednews/2002/

05/10/build/parks/grandcanyon.php?nnn+3>
(July 15, 2002).

24. D. Butcher, p. 200.

25. "Water Pollution," May 4, 1999, <http://www.nature.nps.gov/wrd/twpnps.htm> (July 15, 2002).

26. Roy J. Irwin, *Environmental Contaminants Encyclopedia Oil Spills Entry,* National Park Service, Water Resources Divisions, Fort Collins, Colorado, July 1, 1997, pp. 7, 9, 19, and 37.

Chapter 6. Culture Clash

1. "Kaibab-Paiute Tribe," October 27, 1998, <http://www.itcaonline.com/Tribes/kaibab.htm> (January 23, 2003).

2. Diane Liggett, "NPS Sustainability Efforts Reach for the Stars at Chaco Culture National Historical Park," *Outlook*, June 11, 2002, <http://www.nature.nps.gov/sustainability/Spring_2002/Chaco/Chaco_Outlook.htm> (July 15, 2002).

3. *Management Policies 2001*, NPS D1416, National Park Service, Washington, D.C., December 2000,, p. 89.

4. Ibid., p. 48.

5. "Tribal Preservation Program Helping Tribes Preserve Their Cultural Heritage," April 24, 2001, <http://www2.cr.nps.gov/tribal/tribal_p.htm> (February 20, 2002).

6. *Management Policies 2001*, p. 54.

7. Ibid., p. 94.

8. Russell D. Butcher, *National Parks and Conservation Association: Exploring Our National Historical Parks and Sites* (Niwot, Colo.: Roberts Rinehart Publishers, 1997), pp. 292–293.

•••

9. Ibid., pp. 291–292.

Chapter 7. Safety and the Future

1. Devereux Butcher, *Exploring Our National Parks and Monuments*, Revised Eighth Edition (Boston: The Harvard Common Press, 1986), p. 73.

2. Ibid., p. 13.

3. Ibid., p. 76.

4. Todd Wilkinson, "On the Homefront," *National Parks*, April/May 2002, <http://www.ncpa.org/magazine/2002/april_may/homefront.asp> (June 8, 2002).

5. Ibid.

6. "9.11.01 Remembrance," n.d., <http://www.nps.gov/remembrance/mtrainier/index.html> (January 21, 2003).

7. "Frequently Asked Questions About the National Park Service," updated July 17, 2001, <http://www.nps.gov/pub_aff/e-mail/faqs.htm> (July 14, 2002).

8. Lary M. Dilsaver, ed., *America's National Park System: The Critical Documents*, Introduction: "The National Park System," updated October 25, 2000, <http://www.cr.nps.gov/history/online_books/anps/anps_intro.htm> (November 20, 2001).

9. *2000–2001 Business Plan for Denali National Park and Preserve*, National Park Service, Denali National Park and Preserve, Alaska, p. 1.

10. Ibid., p. 9.

11. Ibid., p. 10.

12. Susannah Zak Figura, "Progress in the Parks," March 1, 2000, <http://www.govexec.com/gpp/0300nps.htm> (February 1, 2002).

13. Ibid.

Glossary

accessibility—The provision of National Park Service (NPS) programs, facilities, and services in ways that include individuals with disabilities, or makes available to those individuals the same benefits available to persons without disabilities.

backcountry—Primitive, undeveloped portions of parks, some of which may be categorized as wilderness.

carrying capacity—The type and level of visitor use that can be accommodated while sustaining the desired resource and visitor experience in a park.

Clean Air Act—The law, most recently amended in 1990, that governs air pollution sources in the United States.

Clean Water Act—The law governing water pollution sources in the United States.

ecosystem—A system formed by the interaction of a community of organisms with their physical environment, considered a unit.

exotic species—Plants or animals that have been brought into an area they are not native to, either by accident or by intent.

fire control policy—Management plan developed by a park that details how it will fight wildland fires and how it will apply prescribed burns.

fire ecology—The study of fire and its effects.

floodplains—Areas along rivers that are routinely flooded with high water.

Leave No Trace (LNT)—Principles and practices that emphasize leaving a place free of human presence; applied to all forms of recreation management within wilderness or backcountry areas.

lightscapes—The state of natural resources and values as they exist in the absence of human-caused light.

National Environmental Policy Act (NEPA)—The law that emphasized the need for environmental planning and community involvement in any action that might have wide environmental consequences.

National Historic Site (NHS)—A site managed by the National Park Service whose value is predominantly historical.

National Monument (NM)—A site managed by the National Park Service, usually commemorating a single entity.

National Park (NP)—A unit in the National Park Service with nationally significant natural resources; also used as a general term for any unit in the National Park Service.

National Park Service (NPS)—An agency under the Department of the Interior whose function is to manage the national parks.

Native Americans—Includes American Indians, Alaskan natives, native peoples of the Caribbean, native Hawaiians, and other native Pacific Islanders.

native species—A species that is indigenous to a certain area; it was not brought in from anywhere else.

naturalist—A type of Park Service employee whose job is to understand and explain the natural and cultural resources; also called an interpreter.

ozone—A special form of oxygen with three oxygen atoms; it is a major form of air pollution in the lower atmosphere but is a beneficial component of the upper atmosphere.

paleontology—The study of fossils.

proclamation authority—The authority of the president of the United States to designate national monuments.

ranger—A type of Park Service employee whose job is to oversee visitor and protective activities.

sacred sites—Certain natural and cultural resources treated by American Indian tribes and Alaska natives as having established religious meaning and as locales of private ceremonial activities.

soundscapes—All the natural, non-human-caused sounds that occur in parks, together with the physical capacity for transmitting natural sounds.

subsistence activities—Activities for supporting life, rather than for recreation.

superintendent—The senior on-site Park Service official in a park.

visibility—The distance visitors are able to see; visibility decreases with increases in air pollution.

visitor—Anyone who uses a park's interpretive and educational services, regardless of where such use occurs (that is, even a visitor to the Web site is considered a Park Service visitor); anyone who enters a national park for recreational purposes.

watershed—A region that drains to a particular body of water (usually named for that body of water).

wetlands—Land or areas (such as swamps) that contain residual moisture.

wilderness—Federal land that has been designated by Congress as a component of the national wilderness preservation system.

woolly adelgid—An exotic pest insect that is inflicting serious damage to the coniferous forests of the Eastern United States.

Further Reading

Gartner, Bob. *Exploring Careers in the National Parks*. New York: Rosen Publishing, 1999.

Muir, John. *Our National Parks* (reprint). San Francisco: Sierra Club Books, 1991.

Peterson, David, editor. *National Parks*. New York: Scholastic, 2001.

Scott, David L., and Kay Woelfel Scott. *Guide to the National Park Areas, Eastern States*. Guilford, Conn.: Globe Pequot Press, 2002.

Swinburne, Stephen R. *Once a Wolf: How Wildlife Biologists Fought to Bring Back the Gray Wolf*. Boston: Houghton Mifflin, 2001.

Internet Addresses

Leave No Trace
<http://www.lnt.org>

National Interagency Fire Center
<http://www.nifc.gov>

National Park Service
<http://www.nps.gov>

Index